Southern Legacies

by
Nancy Patty Walker

Library of Congress Catalogue Card Number 81-92840
ISBN 0-939-11475-5

Wimmer Brothers Books
P.O. Box 18408
Memphis, TN 38118
"Cookbooks of Distinction"™

Introduction

November, 1982

This edition could well be named "Mission Impossible" because at the age of 83, I have finally put it together—and nobody is more surprised than I am.

Southern Legacies was written because of the encouragement of my family (and I might add insistence), and because of my strong feeling that, in this day of fast foods and quick cooking, the old recipes should be preserved. Trying in this book to combine the best of both the new and the old, I have spent many hours and tested many recipes.

The book started back in 1960 when my two daughters, who had married and moved away from home, were making many collect long distance calls with requests for their favorite recipes. As a Christmas labor of love, I typed my first cook book (two copies). The girls found in their Christmas stockings a little red leather book with the title, *Have Book, Will Cook*. They liked the book, the telephone bills went down, and I thought that was sufficient. But as the family grew, there were more requests for the cook book. More recipes were added, and in 1971 my husband had seventy-five copies printed for the family and friends under the name, *Mother's Best*. Then in 1979, as an eightieth birthday present to me, my two sons-in-law had three hundred copies of a revised *Mother's Best* printed. The enthusiastic response to the book encouraged me to develop it further, for I really believe that an attractively served home cooked meal is an integral part of family life and that the old recipes are truly legacies.

In this edition I have left the original notes and postscripts to the family, at their request. Now let me introduce you to my "super" family. Nancy (my older daughter) and her husband, Bill, have two sons, Nick and Kevin. Jeanne (my younger daughter) and her husband, Tommy, have three daughters, Nancy III, Gigi and Olivia, and I am now blessed with a great grandson, Justin, and a great granddaughter, Lylee. So join our family and cook along with us! I hope that you will enjoy the recipes in the book as much as I have enjoyed working them out.

Happy Cooking!

Introductions to the Previous Editions

November, 1960

Well, dears, here they are, Mother's Best, the recipes that I have borrowed, dreamed up and taken liberties with through the past 40 years. I sincerely hope that you will have as much fun cooking for your little ones as I have had, and that these recipes will add a little zest to that cooking.

I realize that in this day of cake mixes, all the recipes that I have included for cakes may seem unnecessary, but remember girls, a cake-mix cake is only a cake, but a homemade cake is Husband Bait!

Merry, merry Christmas and happy cooking!

Mother

November, 1971

P.S. Well, here I am again—can you believe it's been eleven years since the first edition and I'm still young enough to take liberties! The first edition was Mother's Best and this edition is Grandmother's Best. Believe me, it's cheaper than giving recipes long distance.

Here are the "goodies" I've gathered the last few years, so when you think about the freezer, forget it and reach for the little leather book!

Love you,

Grandma

November, 1979

P.P.S. I didn't wait as long for the third edition. You know tomorrow is only a day away, but I'm trying to use today.

This third edition is dedicated to the third generation addition to the family, my adorable great grandson, Justin, who looks like he will always enjoy eating.

Hope you will like the new recipes I've included and that the third will prove to be the charm!

Love you all,

Great Grandma

Acknowledgements

I want to express my appreciation to my friends, who, through the years, have shared their recipes with me. And a special thanks to Henrietta Grayer, my friend and helper for the last forty-two years. Without her encouragement and assistance this book would not have been possible.

Editing: Nancy Walker Stone
William E. Stone

Illustrations: Vanderbeek & Bost Design Studio
Jeanne Walker Wakeman
Thomas O. Wakeman

Photography: Fred Faulk
Vanderbeek & Bost Design Studio
Starkville, Mississippi

Dedication

Dedicated in loving memory to my husband Buz M. Walker Jr., who encouraged me to write my first cookbook and was always my greatest fan.

Table of Contents

Hors d'Oeuvres

Artichoke Dip

1 (14 oz.) can artichoke hearts, drained
1 package creamy Italian salad dressing mix
1 cup Lemon Mayonnaise

Mix salad dressing mix with mayonnaise and blend. Stir in the chopped artichokes and mix well. Serve with crackers.

P.S. You wouldn't believe anything this easy could be so good. Keeps well in the "fridge".

Clam Dip

1 cup sour cream
1 shallot, finely chopped
½ teaspoon salt
Dash pepper
Dash garlic salt
1 teaspoon Worcestershire
Dash hot pepper sauce
1 (6½ oz.) can minced clams

Drain all liquid from clams. Combine clams with other ingredients. Chill. Serve with potato chips.

Horseradish Vegetable Dip

8 oz. cream cheese
1 teaspoon Creole mustard
3 tablespoons heavy cream
2 tablespoons horseradish
Salt and pepper to taste
3 dashes hot pepper sauce
Juice of ½ lemon
¼ cup sour cream
2 tablespoons chopped parsley

Blend all ingredients except parsley. Beat mixture until light and fluffy. Chill and sprinkle with parsley. Serve with broccoli, cauliflower and cherry tomatoes.

Instant Vegetable Dip

½ cup Lemon Mayonnaise
1 teaspoon fresh horseradish
2 teaspoons Dijon mustard
1 tablespoon lime juice

Mix all ingredients. Use as a dip for raw cauliflower, broccoli, celery or turnips.

P.S. Not good with carrots.

Vegetable Dip

1 cup Lemon Mayonnaise
¼ teaspoon ginger
¾ teaspoon curry powder
1 clove garlic, mashed
2 tablespoons lime juice
1 tablespoon honey

Mix well and chill in ice box for 24 hours before using.

P.S. Use as a dip for raw vegetables such as carrot and celery sticks, cauliflower, mushrooms, broccoli, turnips, or whatever you like. It is delicious, and you can make such a pretty tray with colorful fresh vegetables arranged around attractive bowl of dip. Garnish your tray with parsley.

Marion's Cheese Crackers

2 stacks saltines
½ cup butter
6 oz. sharp Cheddar cheese, grated
Red pepper

Spread crackers with butter and place on large cookie sheet. Sprinkle grated cheese and red pepper over crackers. Place under broiler until bubbly. Remove from oven. When oven is cool, set at 150° and bake crackers for 8 hours.

P.S. Melt your butter and put it on with your pastry brush, covering crackers with butter. You can eat these like popcorn!

11

Franzipans

2½ cups flour
1½ teaspoons baking powder
¼ teaspoon salt
4 tablespoon sugar
¾ cup margarine
1 egg, slightly beaten

Sift dry ingredients together and cut in margarine with pastry blender. Add the egg and mix with your hands. Press dough into small Swedish tins, making them as thin as possible. Bake at 450° for 20 minutes.

P.S. Do not try to take these out of the pans with a knife; hit the shell on the side, and they will slide out. These are good filled with chicken, crab or any other meat salad for cocktail parties. They freeze nicely.

P.P.S. If you are serving champagne and want attractive sweet hors d'oeuvres, they make adorable pies. Add 1 tablespoon more sugar to the pastry, fill with any sweet filling and top with whipped cream. I use the lemon filling in the recipe for Angel Pie or any good chocolate filling. If making tiny dessert pies, DON'T FILL THEM UNTIL THE LAST MINUTE; *they are rich and the shells crumble.*

Cheese Straws

1 lb. mild cheese
1 cup butter or margarine
2¾ cups flour
1 teaspoon red pepper

Mix well. Put through your cookie press in strips. Bake at 375° until brown. Sprinkle with salt as soon as you remove from oven.

P.S. These cheese straws are delicious and taste different because the salt is sprinkled on them while they are hot.

Mock Caviar Pie

½ lb. cream cheese with herbs
½ lb. Rondele semi-soft cheese
  spiced with garlic and herbs
1½ cups pitted ripe olives,
  finely chopped
1 tablespoon anchovy, finely
  chopped
Juice of 1 lemon
1 teaspoon anchovy oil
2 hard boiled eggs
Pimiento

Soften and blend cheese together until smooth. Line a 6" soufflé dish with plastic wrap. Oil wrap. Mash cheese in bottom of lined soufflé dish and chill. Turn cheese out on serving plate. Coat top and sides with mixture of chopped olives, anchovy, lemon juice and anchovy oil. Grate the eggs and sprinkle around the top edge of the "pie". Make a flower in the center with 5 strips of pimiento. Garnish plate with parsley. Serve with melba toast rounds.

Cheese Filled Celery

8 oz. cream cheese
8 oz. blue cheese, softened
⅓ cup chopped onions
2 tablespoons sherry
Worcestershire sauce
Bunch of celery

In food processor, blend cream cheese and blue cheese with onions, sherry and a dash of Worcestershire sauce. Transfer to pastry tube fitted with ½" top.

Remove and discard outer blemished stalks of celery. Rinse, pulling each stalk away from heart without separating from base. Pat dry. Starting with inner stalks, fill each stalk with cheese mixture. Re-form bunch. Wrap tightly in plastic wrap and chill for 2 hours. Slice crossways in ¼" slices and serve cold.

Lemons kept at room temperature will yield more juice —

Cheese Roll

3 oz. cream cheese
2 cups grated *sharp* cheese
1 jar Roquefort cheese spread
1 tablespoon Durkee's
  Dressing
Worcestershire sauce
2 large cloves of garlic,
  crushed
Mayonnaise
Salt, black pepper, red pepper
  to taste
Paprika

Combine first six ingredients with enough mayonnaise to make the mixture workable. Season to taste. Roll into a cylinder, 2 inches in diameter and dust completely with paprika. Place in refrigerator until ready to serve.

Note: If you are using a commercial mayonnaise, add a little lemon juice. For cocktail parties, garnish serving plate with parsley, serve with crackers, and let your guests spread their own. This keeps in the ice box for weeks.

Cream Cheese Pine Cone

1¼ cups whole almonds
  (unblanched)
8 oz. cream cheese
½ cup mayonnaise
5 slices bacon, crisp and
  crumbled (optional)
1 tablespoon finely chopped
  onion
½ teaspoon dill weed
Pepper to taste

Spread almonds in a shallow pan. Bake at 300° for 15 minutes. Combine other ingredients and mix until smooth. Chill. Place mixture on wax paper, cover with another piece of wax paper and shape into pine cone shape. Chill again. Slip onto a plate and, beginning at the narrow end, press almonds at slight angle into cheese mixture in rows. Overlap rows until cheese is covered. Garnish with pine sprig. Serve with party crackers.

P.S. This is not much trouble and it always makes a hit at a party.

Cheese Straws

1 cup butter
1 lb. sharp cheese, grated
2 cups sifted flour
1 teaspoon baking powder
1 teaspoon salt
1 tablespoon cold water
 (optional)
Red pepper to taste

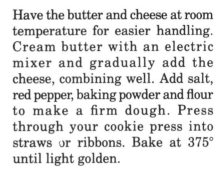

Have the butter and cheese at room temperature for easier handling. Cream butter with an electric mixer and gradually add the cheese, combining well. Add salt, red pepper, baking powder and flour to make a firm dough. Press through your cookie press into straws or ribbons. Bake at 375° until light golden.

Note: These are better if you don't use the water, but the dough is so stiff I have trouble getting it through the cookie press if I don't use it. I think the secret is to have your butter and cheese soft. I like these made with very sharp cheese but that is a matter of taste.

Mushrooms in Vermouth

4 (4 oz.) cans button
 mushrooms, drained
½ cup dry vermouth
½ cup olive oil
½ cup red wine vinegar
1 clove garlic crushed
2 tablespoons chopped onion
1 tablespoon basil leaves
1 teaspoon salt
½ teaspoon pepper
½ teaspoon sugar
½ teaspoon dry mustard

Put mushrooms in two 8 oz. jars with tight fitting lids. Combine all other ingredients, and stir until well mixed. Pour over mushrooms. Seal and store in refrigerator up to two months. Serve as an hors d'oeuvre or as a garnish for cold meats.

P.S. Some people like to add a little curry powder. I don't.

15

Chicken Liver Pâté

2½ lbs. chicken livers
¾ cup butter
1 large onion (sliced)
½ cup Cognac
1 teaspoon salt
1 teaspoon pepper
Hot pepper sauce to taste

Sauté livers until tender in ½ of butter. Put cooked livers, remaining butter and other ingredients in bowl of food processor. Process until well blended. Put into buttered mold and refrigerate overnight. Unmold and cover with following glaze:

Glaze:

1 tablespoon gelatine
1 tablespoon water
1 cup white wine
½ teaspoon tarragon
½ teaspoon chopped parsley
Pimiento or sliced olives

Soak gelatine in water. Add white wine. Dissolve over heat. Add tarragon and chopped parsley. Pour a layer of glaze over pâté. Put into ice box until it hardens. Repeat until all of glaze has been used and mold is covered. Decorate with olives, pimiento, etc. Serve with party crackers.

Mushroom and Avocado Canapés

½ cup olive oil
1 tablespoon tarragon vinegar
1 tablespoon minced parsley
1 garlic clove, crushed
1 teaspoon salt
½ teaspoon pepper
1 lb. fresh medium sized
    mushroom caps
2 avocados, peeled and sliced
Juice of 1 lemon
Pimiento
Parsley

Combine oil, vinegar, parsley, garlic and seasonings. Add mushrooms. Place mixture in a plastic bag, squeeze out all of air and tie securely. Marinate overnight in "fridge". Purée avocado with lemon juice and spoon into each mushroom cap. Transfer stuffed mushrooms to chilled serving platter. Garnish with strips of pimiento and chopped parsley.

P.S. Try these, they are different and very good.

Shrimp Butter Ball

1 cup cooked, finely chopped
   shrimp
½ cup butter, softened
1 tablespoon sherry
1 teaspoon Worcestershire
1 tablespoon grated onion
Juice of 1 lemon
Dash garlic salt
⅛ teaspoon red pepper
¾ cup finely chopped fresh
   parsley

Cream butter and add all ingredients except parsley. Combine well. Chill and roll into a ball. Cover with half of the parsley. Put in center of serving dish and surround with remaining parsley. Chill until ready to serve. Serve with unsalted crackers.

Shrimp Mousse

2 tablespoons gelatine
½ cup water
1 (10 oz.) can tomato soup
8 oz. cream cheese
1 cup Lemon Mayonnaise
1 lb. cooked, chopped shrimp
¾ cup chopped celery
¼ cup chopped green pepper
1 tablespoon grated onion
1 tablespoon Durkee's
   Dressing
¼ teaspoon salt
1 teaspoon Worcestershire
Juice of 1 lemon
3 dashes of hot pepper sauce

Soak gelatine in cold water. Heat undiluted soup, add gelatine and stir until dissolved. Add cream cheese to mixture and stir until melted. Cool. Beat in food processor until smooth. Add mayonnaise, shrimp, vegetables and seasonings. Mix well and pour into oiled fish mold. Chill until firm. Unmold on serving platter. Use olive slices for eyes and pimiento slices for scales and tail. Garnish and serve with melba toast rounds.

Note: This is a pretty hors d'oeuvre for a large party. It also is nice to serve as a salad with Lemon Mayonnaise. As a salad, it will serve 8.

a pan of boiling water and vinegar on back burner will prevent fish odor —

Martha's Tomato Soup Surprise

2 tablespoons unflavored
  gelatine
2 tablespoons water
1 (10 oz.) can tomato soup,
  undiluted
6 oz. cream cheese
½ cup cold water
1 cup chopped celery
1 cup chopped nuts
1 cup mayonnaise
1 cup boiled shrimp, chopped
Small bottle sliced stuffed
  olives (optional)
1 tablespoon lemon juice
½ teaspoon HOT pepper sauce
1 teaspoon Worcestershire
  sauce
Salt and pepper to taste

Soak gelatine in water. Heat tomato soup, add cream cheese and stir until smooth. Add gelatine. Remove from heat and stir in other ingredients. Chill in small molds until firm.

P.S. Plastic egg containers work well as molds. Fill ½ full with the salad. Chill until firm. Unmold on melba toast rounds or party crackers. Pass a platter of small salads garnished with parsley for an hors d'oeuvre. This is attractive to serve.

Marinated Shrimp

5 lbs. shrimp, peeled and
  deveined

Marinade:
⅔ cup vinegar
2 medium onions, chopped
  fine
½ teaspoon red pepper
1⅓ cups salad oil
2 cloves garlic, crushed
Salt to taste

Boil shrimp in your usual seasonings. Drain and cool. Marinate shrimp in sauce in the ice box 24 hours. Serve chilled.

Note: These are delicious for big cocktail parties.

Cheese Balls

2 cups sharp cheese, grated
1 cup butter
2 cups crispy rice cereal
2 cups flour
1 teaspoon salt
1 teaspoon red pepper

Mix together and make into little balls. Flatten slightly with a fork and bake at 375° until brown.

Note: These are a favorite of my daughter Nancy. I always have some on hand when she comes to visit. They are easy to make and keep a long time in a cake tin.

Shrimp Boats

1 package won ton skins
8 medium sized mushrooms
2 tablespoons butter
2 tablespoons lemon juice
1½ cups cooked shrimp
½ cup chopped celery
¼ cup chopped green pepper
2 green onions
3 tablespoons chopped
  parsley
1 clove garlic, puréed
1 teaspoon Worcestershire
Hot pepper sauce
Salt and pepper
2 teaspoons cornstarch
¼ cup half and half cream

If using frozen won ton skins, take from freezer a few minutes before making filling. Sauté mushrooms in butter and lemon juice. Remove mushrooms, reserving butter in skillet. Place mushrooms, shrimp, celery, green pepper, parsley and onions in bowl of food processor. Mince by turning off and on quickly. Do not mince too fine. Add garlic, Worcestershire and several dashes of hot pepper sauce to mixture. Salt and pepper to taste. In skillet with butter, stir in cornstarch and add half and half. Whisk until thickened. Add enough to shrimp mixture to make mixture hold together.

Place a heaping teaspoonful of shrimp mixture in center of each won ton skin. Moisten edges of skin and fold opposite corner over to form a triangle. Press to seal edges. Pinch the points together. Deep fry in vegetable oil heated to 375° for about 2 minutes. Fry only a few at a time. Drain on paper towel and sprinkle with salt. Serve hot.

Bacon Crisps

Parmesan cheese, grated
Thin salted crackers
Bacon slices cut in half

Put heaps of cheese on top of each cracker. Wrap in bacon. Put on rack of broiler pan and bake at 200° for 2 hours.

P.S. These are good hot or cold and freeze well.

Bacon Curls

Thin-sliced bacon strips
Thin salted crackers

Have your butcher slice bacon as thin as possible, on the ½ cutter. Divide the crackers and wrap a slice of bacon around each. Bake in 350° oven until brown.

Note: This is my favorite hors d'oeuvre, but it's hard to find a butcher to slice your bacon this thin.

Hot Broccoli Dip

1 medium onion, chopped
¼ lb. fresh mushrooms, chopped
3 stalks celery, chopped
3 tablespoons butter
6 oz. garlic cheese
10 oz. cooked chopped broccoli
1 (10 oz.) can cream of mushroom soup
Hot pepper sauce
Worcestershire sauce

Sauté onions, mushrooms and celery in butter. Melt cheese in top of double boiler. Blend in all other ingredients. Serve in chafing dish, with corn chips or party crackers.

P.S. A good hot hors d'oeuvre!

Cheese Biscuits

½ lb. very sharp cheese,
   grated
½ cup butter
1 cup flour
1 teaspoon salt
¼ teaspoon red pepper
⅔ cup finely chopped nuts

Cream butter and cheese, add flour, salt, red pepper and nuts. Shape into very small biscuits and bake at 375° until light brown. .

P.S. These will keep for a long time.

Cheese Olives Mildred

1¼ cups flour
½ cup margarine
10 oz. sharp cheese, grated
Dash hot sauce
4 oz. bottle of stuffed olives

Make pastry with flour, margarine, cheese and hot sauce. Roll out about ¼" thick. Cut pieces and wrap around stuffed olives until covered. Put on greased cookie sheet in 350° oven and bake until brown. Serve hot.

P.S. These taste awfully good with a "Coke" when you are playing bridge. Good for cocktail parties, too.

Cheese Puffs

¼ lb. grated cheese (1 cup)
¼ cup softened butter
½ cup all-purpose flour
¼ teaspoon salt
½ teaspoon paprika
24 large stuffed olives

About 24 hours before serving, blend cheese with butter. Stir in dry ingredients and mix well. Wrap olives in about 1 teaspoon of dough, covering each olive completely. Place on ungreased cookie sheet and refrigerate. About ½ hour before serving, bake puffs in 400° oven for 10-14 minutes.

P.S. Great for cocktail parties!

21

Toasted Cheese Squares

8 oz. cream cheese
6 green onions, finely chopped
6 tablespoons Lemon
   Mayonnaise
6 drops HOT pepper sauce
Thin-sliced bread
Butter
Parmesan cheese

Trim crusts from bread and cut slices into four squares. Butter and toast on one side. Mix other ingredients and spread on the untoasted side. Sprinkle with Parmesan cheese and bake at 350° until brown.

P.S. These freeze well. Reheat when ready to serve.

P.P.S. A variation of this recipe is to follow the recipe for Crabmeat Dip and spread it on the toasted squares before cooking.

P.P.P.S. These are a variation of Deviled Ham-Cheese Squares.

Sardine Rounds

1 (3¾ oz.) can boneless
   sardines
2 tablespoons lemon juice
1 tablespoon cream
½ teaspoon dry mustard
1 tablespoon mayonnaise
Pepper to taste
Few drops of HOT pepper
   sauce
Toast rounds
Capers or olives

Drain sardines and mash with a fork. Mix with seasonings. Spread on toast rounds and garnish with capers or sliced olives.

P.S. I butter my toast rounds and cook them until very dry.

Chicken Livers and Mushrooms

1 lb. chicken livers
1 (8 oz.) can button
 mushrooms, drained

Marinade:
½ cup cooking oil
½ cup soy sauce
Juice of 2 lemons
2 tablespoons Worcestershire
 sauce
1 clove garlic, crushed
1 teaspoon salt
Hot pepper sauce to taste

Wash the chicken livers, cut in halves and remove membranes. Mix ingredients for the marinade. Put livers and mushrooms in marinade, cover and leave in refrigerator overnight. When ready to cook, remove livers with a slotted spoon and put in baking pan. Broil, turn once and baste with a little of the marinade to keep moist. Put livers, mushrooms and the remaining marinade in a chafing dish. Serve warm, with melba toast or party crackers.

P.S. This makes an interesting hors d'oeuvre.

Deviled Ham-Cheese Squares

Thin-sliced bread
3 oz. cream cheese
1 (4½ oz.) can deviled ham
2 green onions, finely chopped
Mayonnaise
2 teaspoons Worcestershire
 sauce
1 clove garlic, mashed
1 tablespoon India relish

Cut crust from bread. Cut each slice into four squares and toast one side of each square.

 In mixing bowl, mix cream cheese, deviled ham, green onions, and enough mayonnaise to soften. Add Worcestershire, garlic and India relish. Mix well and put a spoonful on untoasted side of each of the bread squares. Put squares on baking sheet in middle of oven and slightly brown under broiler.

P.S. Serve hot and you have an hors d'oeuvre that is a little different (and very easy to make). Or freeze uncooked and cook as you need them.

23

Crabmeat Dip

6 oz. fresh or canned crab
  meat
Onion juice to taste
1 tablespoon Worcestershire
  sauce
½ cup Lemon Mayonnaise
Dash red pepper
Salt and pepper
1 egg white, stiffly beaten

To crab meat, add onion juice, Worcestershire sauce, mayonnaise, red pepper and salt and pepper to taste. Mix and fold the egg white in last. Bake at 400° for 10 minutes. Serve in chafing dish, with rounds of melba toast.

P.S. You'll like this even if you think you don't like mayonnaise, and it's as easy as can be!

Mushroom Pastries

1 cup fresh mushrooms
2 tablespoons butter
1 tablespoon flour
½ cup finely chopped green
  onions
½ teaspoon salt
¼ teaspoon thyme
1 egg yolk
Cream Cheese Pastry

Sauté the mushrooms in 1 tablespoon of the butter. Drain and chop fine. Cream 1 tablespoon butter with the flour and add to mushrooms with the onions, salt, thyme and egg yolk. Mix well. Roll pastry and cut into small rounds. Put 1 teaspoon filling on half of each round. Fold over and press edges. Bake at 375° until brown.

P.S. Different and good!

Cocktail Meat Balls

1 lb. ground beef
1 egg
Cooking oil

Mix the meat and egg and form into small balls. Brown in skillet in small amount of cooking oil. Remove from skillet and place in chafing dish. Pour the sauce over the meat balls and keep warm. Serve with toothpicks.

Sauce:

2 tablespoons butter
1 onion, chopped fine
1 clove garlic, minced
½ cup chopped celery
¾ cup water
1 cup catsup
2 tablespoons vinegar
2 tablespoons lemon juice
2 tablespoons Worcestershire
  sauce
2 tablespoons brown sugar
1 teaspoon dry mustard
1 teaspoon salt
1 teaspoon pepper

Wilt the onion, garlic and celery in the butter. Add the other ingredients and bring to a boil.

Pecan Teasers

12 strips thinly sliced bacon
½ cup chopped pecans
1 cup grated sharp cheese
1 teaspoon grated onion
½ cup mayonnaise
½ teaspoon salt
12 slices thin white bread

Cook bacon until crisp, drain and crumble. Blend with other ingredients. Remove crusts from bread. Cut each slice into four squares and spread mixture on top of each square. Bake at 350° until lightly brown.

P.S. These freeze well and are very good! Freeze uncooked, remove from freezer, bake and serve.

Margy's Hot Hors d'oeuvre Rolls

1 cup bean sprouts, chopped slightly
½ lb. ground beef
½ cup water chestnuts, chopped
2 tablespoons finely chopped onion
1 envelope beef flavored mushroom mix
2 packages of refrigerator crescent rolls

In skillet, combine first five ingredients. Brown well. Separate dough and cut each square into halves. Put 1 tablespoon mixture on each square and roll up. Moisten edge to seal. Bake at 375° until brown.

P.S. If you want to freeze these, partially bake before freezing and finish baking just before serving. These are really delicious.

Rumaki

10 chicken livers
10 slices bacon
1 small can water chestnuts
¼ cup honey
½ cup soy sauce
½ teaspoon grated fresh ginger
1 teaspoon garlic, minced

Make marinade of soy sauce and honey. Flavor with ginger and garlic.

Mix marinade in 13x9x2″ pan. Clean chicken livers and separate in half for bite sized pieces. Cut bacon slices in half. Slice water chestnuts into small pieces, 3 or 4 slices per nut. Wrap in bacon one water chestnut slice with each piece of liver and fasten with a toothpick. Place in marinade for 5 hours. Charcoal on grill for 15 to 20 minutes or bake on rack over a shallow pan in 375° oven until bacon is crisp. Turn for even cooking.

P.S. Double recipe for cocktail party. Serve in chafing dish. One of my favorites.

Sausage Balls

½ lb. very sharp cheese
1 lb. HOT sausage
3½ or 4 cups biscuit mix

Melt cheese in double boiler. Add sausage, take off stove and blend thoroughly. Add biscuit mix until a firm dough is formed. Form in firm balls about the size of a walnut. Bake at 350° until brown.

P.S. If hot sausage is not available, season regular sausage liberally with crushed red pepper.

P.P.S. I keep these in the freezer for unexpected company. Freeze in plastic bags and bake as needed. These are not good unless you use HOT sausage (and I do mean HOT) sausage.

Sausage Pinwheels

2 cups flour
2 teaspoons baking powder
½ teaspoon salt
½ cup corn meal
4 tablespoons shortening
¾ cup milk, approximately
1 lb. uncooked HOT sausage

Sift the flour, baking powder and salt into a bowl. Stir in the corn meal. Cut in the shortening until the mixture resembles coarse meal. Add milk until you have a pliable dough. Roll into rectangular shape about ⅛" thick. Spread with the sausage and roll the dough from the long edge, jelly-roll fashion. Dampen the edge with water to seal. Wrap in wax paper and refrigerate overnight. When you are ready to serve, cut roll in slices ¼" thick and bake at 400° until brown. Serve hot.

Artichoke Delights

⅓ cup finely chopped onion
1 clove garlic, crushed
2 tablespoons oil
4 eggs
1 (14 oz.) can artichoke hearts,
  drained and chopped
¼ cup bread crumbs
½ lb. Swiss cheese
2 tablespoons minced parsley
½ teaspoon salt
½ teaspoon oregano
Dash of HOT pepper sauce
Pepper

Grease 7x11″ baking dish. In skillet, sauté onion and garlic in oil. In mixing bowl, beat eggs until frothy. Add the artichokes, onion mixture, crumbs, cheese, parsley and seasonings. Put mix in baking dish and bake at 325° for 25-30 minutes, or until set when lightly touched. Let cool slightly and cut in 1½″ squares before serving.

Note: This can be baked and refrigerated. Reheat at 325° for 10 minutes before cutting into squares and serving.

Bourbon Wieners

1 package all-beef wieners
½ cup Bourbon
½ cup chili sauce
½ cup brown sugar, scant
1 tablespoon honey

Cut wieners into bite sized pieces. Combine the other ingredients, pour over wieners and simmer for 1 hour. Pour into chafing dish and serve hot.

P.S. Try these. They are great!

Soups,
Salads and Sauces

Cream of Broccoli Soup

4 cups chicken broth
1 onion, chopped
1 large potato, chopped
5 spears fresh broccoli,
   chopped
2 tablespoons fresh parsley,
   chopped
2 stalks celery, chopped
2 bay leaves
½ teaspoon basil leaves,
   crushed
½ teaspoon salt
¼ teaspoon pepper
⅛ teaspoon hot pepper sauce,
   more if you like
½ pint heavy cream
Sour cream for garnish

Cook vegetables in chicken broth and seasonings until soft. Remove bay leaves and beat mixture with metal blade in food processor until thoroughly blended. Put mixture in pot, add cream and heat. Serve in soup bowls with a heaping teaspoon of sour cream in center.

P.S. If you are dieting as usual, omit cream and substitute a cup of chicken broth. It's not as good, but it's not as fattening either.

P.P.S. Other vegetables can be substituted for broccoli, like zucchini, etc. A great way to clean the refrigerator!

Potato Soup

3 cups leeks
3 cups potatoes
3 cups chicken broth
1 teaspoon salt
2 teaspoons Worcestershire
½ teaspoon pepper
½ teaspoon celery salt
¼ teaspoon garlic salt
2 tablespoons dry white wine
½ pint heavy cream
2 tablespoons chopped
   parsley

Cook all ingredients except cream and parsley until vegetables are tender. Beat with metal blade in food processor until thoroughly blended. Put mixture in pot, add cream and heat. Serve in soup bowls with parsley sprinkled on top.

P.S. Served chilled this is a delicious Vichyssoise.

French Onion Soup

¼ cup butter
4 cups thinly sliced onions
1 teaspoon sugar
1 teaspoon salt
⅛ teaspoon pepper
3 tablespoons all purpose
 flour
2½ cups beef broth
2 cups water
2 tablespoons sherry
1 cup slivered Gruyere cheese
French bread
Butter
Parmesan cheese

Melt butter in heavy saucepan, add onions, cover and cook over low heat for 15 minutes. Uncover, stir in sugar, salt and pepper. Cook over medium heat until onions are golden brown. Remove from heat. Stir in flour, add broth, water and sherry, stirring constantly until blended. Simmer about 30 minutes. Just before serving stir in the Gruyere cheese. Toast French bread on both sides, butter and sprinkle with Parmesan cheese. Pour soup in oven proof bowls, float toast on top and run under broiler until cheese is browned.

P.S. I knew I didn't throw away this recipe! This is for Tommy.

When a broth, or soup, is too
salty, add slices raw potato —

Avocado Salad

4 medium sized avocados,
  ripe but firm
3 medium sized tomatoes
½ cup chopped celery
¼ cup chopped green onion
¼ cup chopped green pepper
3 tablespoons finely chopped
  parsley
Lemon Mayonnaise

Peel avocados and cut into small cubes. Peel and dice tomatoes. Combine both with other vegetables. Add enough mayonnaise to blend ingredients well. Chill and serve on lettuce with a wedge of lime and a dash of curry powder.

P.S. We first had this salad in 1975 when we were on safari in Kenya. I had never thought of using avocados this way but it makes a good salad.

To ripen avocados, or tomatoes, put in a brown bag in a dark place —

Bean Sprout Salad

½ lb. fresh bean sprouts
2 teaspoons vegetable oil
1 egg
½ cup chopped green onions
1 tablespoon vinegar
1 teaspoon sugar
1 tablespoon sesame oil

Put colander in larger pan. Pour boiling water over bean sprouts in colander. Leave in water 2 minutes. Pick up colander and drain. Rinse immediately in ice water. Set aside to chill. Fry egg like a pancake in vegetable oil and cut into thin strips. Mix bean sprouts, onion and egg strips. Mix vinegar, sesame oil and sugar in separate bowl. When ready to serve, combine. Serves 6-8.

P.S. As Bill says, salads don't HAVE to be uninteresting. This is a change from the "ole reliable" green salad.

Beet Salad

2 envelopes gelatine
¼ cup water
2 (14 oz.) cans sliced beets
½ cup sugar
1½ teaspoons salt
½ cup white vinegar
1½ cups chopped celery
2 tablespoons horseradish

Soften gelatine in water. Drain beets, and set liquid aside. Add enough water to beet liquid to make 3 cups. Add sugar, salt and vinegar. Bring to a boil and add gelatine. Cool. Chop beets. Fold beets, celery and horseradish into gelatine mixture. Pour into individual molds and chill until firm. Serves 6-8.

Note: This is good served with 1 tablespoon cottage cheese and 1 teaspoon Lemon Mayonnaise with each serving. I like this with ham or any cold sliced meat.

Bing Cherry Salad

3 tablespoons gelatine
2 cups orange juice
1 (16 oz.) can Bing cherries
1 cup sugar
1½ cups sherry
1 (8 oz.) can crushed pineapple
Small stuffed olives, sliced

Soak gelatine in ½ cup orange juice. Put rest of orange juice, juice from cherries and sugar in a sauce pan and bring to a boil. Dissolve gelatine in the hot mixture. When cool, add sherry, cherries which have been pitted and chopped, pineapple, and olives. Pour into individual molds or a square pan and chill until set. Serve with Lemon Mayonnaise. Serves 8.

P.S. This salad is especially good with cold sliced turkey or ham.

Brutus Salad

2 tablespoons lemon juice
1 tablespoon wine vinegar
2 cloves garlic
2 small to medium size heads
  of Romaine lettuce
½ cup croutons
⅓ cup salad oil
¼ cup crumbled blue cheese
2 tablespoons grated
  Parmesan cheese
Salt and pepper

Combine the lemon juice and vinegar in a small glass. Mash the garlic and add to the lemon juice mixture. Let garlic remain in the liquid at least 2 hours, then remove. Rub the salad bowl with garlic. Tear the Romaine into pieces. Put all ingredients in a large salad bowl, toss thoroughly and season with salt and pepper.

P.S. This is like a Caesar salad but different enough to need another name!

Jellied Chicken Salad

1 chicken, approximately
  4 lbs.
1 cup chopped celery
7 hard boiled eggs, mashed
1½ envelopes gelatine
1½ cups chicken stock, hot
½ cup Lemon Mayonnaise
6½ oz. bottle Durkee's
  dressing
6 tablespoons lemon juice
1 teaspoon grated lemon rind
Salt, pepper and hot pepper
  sauce to taste

Boil the chicken until tender. Skim fat from broth and put broth aside for use in salad. Chop up chicken, discarding all bones, skin and gristle. Mix chicken, celery and eggs. Dissolve gelatine in the hot chicken stock. Cool. Mix mayonnaise, Durkee's dressing, lemon juice and lemon rind with chicken. Add gelatine and mix. Season *well* with salt, pepper and hot pepper sauce (tends to be bland, otherwise). Pour into molds and refrigerate until firm. Serves 12.

Note: I use individual molds. I serve each individual mold on a lettuce leaf and garnish with parsley and pimiento. Pretty!

Club Salad

4 tablespoons gelatine
1 (20 oz.) can crushed
  pineapple
1 pint boiling water
¾ cup sugar
1 pint heavy cream, whipped
1 cup nuts
6 oz. maraschino cherries
1 pint Lemon Mayonnaise
1 teaspoon salt

Soften gelatine in juice drained from pineapple. Add boiling water and sugar. Stir to dissolve. Cool. When mixture begins to congeal, add mayonnaise and other ingredients. Pour into mold or large flat pan that has been rinsed in cold water. Refrigerate until firm.

P.S. Not bad and easy to make. Cut in blocks and garnish with a cherry. Serves the whole club.

Corned Beef Mold

1 envelope gelatine
¼ cup water
½ cup tomato juice
¼ teaspoon salt
2 cups chopped celery
1 tablespoon chopped onion
1 tablespoon lemon juice
¼ cup water
½ cup chopped cucumber
1 cup Lemon Mayonnaise
1 (12 oz.) can corned beef

Soak gelatine in water. Heat tomato juice and dissolve gelatine in hot juice. Mix other ingredients, add gelatine and chill until thickness of egg whites. Shred the corned beef and stir it into the gelatine mixture. Chill until set. Unmold on lettuce and serve with Lemon Mayonnaise. Serves 8.

P.S. This makes a good summer supper with an asparagus or green bean casserole and a fresh fruit cup.

Slightly over-season congealed or frozen recipes —

Cucumber Freeze in Avocado

2 medium sized cucumbers,
   unpared
1 cup sour cream
¼ cup lime juice
¼ cup sugar
1 teaspoon salt
2 egg whites
4 avocados

Cut unpared cucumbers in halves, remove and discard seeds. Grate the cucumbers into a bowl. Stir in sour cream, lime juice, sugar and salt. Beat egg whites until stiff and fold into the cucumber mixture. Turn into 2 refrigerator trays and put in freezer. When mixture begins to freeze around the edges, turn it into a chilled bowl and beat well. Return to trays and freeze. Spoon the frozen mixture into peeled avocado halves and serve on lettuce leaves. Garnish with a cucumber slice and a wedge of lime. Serves 8.

P.S. This makes me wish I could eat cucumbers! A frosty salad for a hot day.

Frozen Fruit Salad

17 oz. can apricots
17 oz. can fruit cocktail
¼ cup maraschino cherries
1 banana
10 marshmallows
2 oranges, in sections
¼ cup Lemon Mayonnaise
1 cup heavy cream, whipped
1 tablespoon grated orange
   rind

Drain most of juice from canned fruit. Chop banana fine, add to fruit with chopped marshmallows, cherries and oranges. Mix mayonnaise, whipped cream and orange rind and add to fruit mixture. Freeze in a milk carton and serve in slices. Serves 12 with some to spare.

Note: If I have fresh peaches, I add a chopped peach. This is your favorite, Nancy!

Fancy Fruit Salad

1 package lemon flavored
  gelatine
1 cup hot water
1 (10 oz.) package frozen
  mixed fruit, thawed
½ cup white seedless grapes
2 chopped peaches

Dissolve gelatine in hot water. Put in refrigerator until it begins to thicken. Add mixed fruit, grapes and peaches and pour into molds. Refrigerate until firm. Unmold and serve on lettuce leaves with following dressing. Serves 8.

Dressing:

2 egg yolks
1 cup sugar
Pinch of salt
½ cup orange or pineapple
  juice
1½ tablespoons lemon juice
½ pint heavy cream, whipped

Beat egg yolks with sugar and salt, using a wire whisk. Add the fruit juices and cook in double boiler until thickened. Cool. Fold in whipped cream. Chill before serving over molded salads.

Nina's Frozen Fruit Salad

16 oz. cream cheese
1 pint sour cream
¾ cup sugar
2 (16 oz.) cans black cherries,
  drained
1 cup crushed pineapple,
  drained
12 oz. miniature
  marshmallows
1 cup chopped nuts
2 (10 oz.) packages frozen
  strawberries (with juice)

Fluff the cream cheese with a fork and add the other ingredients. Mix well and freeze in 7x11" pan. Cut into squares to serve. Can be frozen in individual molds. Thaw a few minutes before serving. Serves 14-16.

P.S. I usually cut this recipe in half.

To frost grapes, dip in beaten egg white then lightly roll in granulated sugar —

Green Grape Salad

2 lbs. seedless grapes
1 cup sour cream
White crème de cacao

Wash the grapes and mix with the sour cream. Put in icebox for several hours. Serve on lettuce leaves. Pour 2 tablespoons liqueur over each serving.

P.S. A delicious refreshing salad for a hot summer day. Or you can serve as a dessert. I serve in dessert bowls and add 1 teaspoon light brown sugar over each serving before adding the liqueur.

Gourmet Salad

1 (10 oz.) package frozen artichoke hearts
1 package Italian dressing mix
8 oz. canned sliced mushrooms
1 package lemon flavored gelatine
1 tablespoon diced pimiento

Cook artichoke hearts in water until tender, drain and, if whole, cut in halves. In large bowl prepare salad dressing per package directions, add artichokes and mushrooms. Marinate at least one hour, remove from marinade, drain. Prepare gelatine with 1¾ cups water. Refrigerate until gelatine is beginning to thicken. Add artichokes, mushrooms and pimiento and pour into 4 cup mold or individual molds. Refrigerate until firmly set. Unmold and serve on bed of lettuce on chilled platter. Garnish with parsley and slices of pimiento. Serves 6-8.

Grated Carrot Salad

1 (8 oz.) can crushed pineapple
½ cup orange juice
   (approximately)
1 package lemon flavored
   gelatine
¾ cup hot water, scant
1 cup grated carrots
1 tablespoon grated orange
   rind

Dissolve the gelatine in hot water. Cool. Drain all juice from pineapple and add enough orange juice to make one cup. Add fruit juice, carrots, pineapple and orange rind to gelatine. Mix well and pour into individual molds. Serves 6-8.

P.S. Do not use more than 1¾ cups of liquid or salad will not be firm.

P.P.S. This is one salad Dad liked. It tastes so good, he didn't notice it had the dreaded carrot in it.

Spiced Grape Salad

1 (17 oz.) can spiced grapes
Pineapple juice
1 package lemon flavored
   gelatine
1 teaspoon unflavored
   gelatine
½ cup stuffed olives, sliced
1 cup diced celery
1 cup chopped nuts

Drain grapes and save liquid. Add pineapple juice to grape liquid to make 1¾ cups liquid and bring to a boil. Add gelatines to the hot juice. Chill until mixture begins to thicken. Place a layer of sliced olives in the bottom of a mold, add grapes, celery and nuts. Carefully pour the gelatine mixture into the mold. Put in refrigerator until firm. Unmold on bed of lettuce on serving platter. Garnish platter with celery tops and whole stuffed olives. Serves 8.

Note: This is a delicious salad to serve with meats. It can be made with plain white grapes but is better with spiced grapes.

39

Mandarin Orange Salad

1 package orange flavored
  gelatine
3 oz. frozen, unsweetened
  orange juice
1 cup + 2 tablespoons boiling
  water
1 (11 oz.) can mandarin
  oranges, drained
4 oz. water chestnuts, drained
  and chopped
1 teaspoon grated orange rind

Dissolve gelatine in boiling water and add frozen orange juice and orange rind. Mix oranges and water chestnuts and divide between 6 individual gelatine molds. When gelatine mixture is cool, pour into molds, stirring with a fork so that all fruit is covered. Put in refrigerator until firm. Unmold on lettuce leaves and refrigerate again until ready to serve. Serves 6.

P.S. This is a good salad with meat because it is a little tart. The water chestnuts are a pleasant surprise.

Orange Sherbet Salad

2 packages orange flavored
  gelatine
1 cup boiling water
1 pint orange sherbet
1 (11 oz.) can mandarin
  oranges, drained
1 cup heavy cream, whipped

Dissolve gelatine in boiling water. Add sherbet and mix well. When partially set, add mandarin oranges and fold in whipped cream. Pour into 1½ quart ring mold. Chill. Unmold on chilled platter. Garnish with sprigs of mint. Serves 8.

P.S. Pretty when molded in a fancy gelatine mold and served at the table.

Cheese Balls in Aspic

Aspic:

1½ envelopes gelatine
1 (10 oz.) can beef consommé
1½ cups vegetable juice
1 tablespoon sugar
1 teaspoon Worcestershire
    sauce
2 tablespoons vinegar
2 teaspoons seasoning salt
1 dash pepper sauce

Soak gelatine in ¼ cup consommé for about 5 minutes. Heat remaining consommé and pour over gelatine. Stir until gelatine is well dissolved. Add remaining ingredients. Set bowl aside and cool until thickened, stirring occasionally to keep from setting. Use individual molds, place 3 cheese balls in each mold and fill with cooled aspic. Chill until set. Unmold and serve on salad greens. Serves 8.

Cheese Balls:

8 oz. cream cheese
3 teaspoons horseradish
8 stuffed olives, slivered
½ cup chopped nuts

Soften the cream cheese and stir in other ingredients. Make into small balls and chill.

P.S. This is a little different and good with roast or steaks. I always toast my pecans—just don't like "soggy" pecans.

Pear Salad

6 oz. cream cheese
2 tablespoons cream,
    approximately
1 teaspoon grated orange rind
2 tablespoons chopped
    crystallized ginger
4 tablespoons slivered
    almonds
8 canned pears

Mix cream with cream cheese until soft. Add orange rind, ginger and almonds. Mix thoroughly and place between pear halves. Serve on lettuce leaves. Serves 4.

Note: This is especially good with roast lamb. I like to stand the pears upright, brush them with red food coloring and put a mint leaf in the top of each pear. Very pretty!

Layered Aspic

Avocado Layer:

1 envelope unflavored gelatine
3 tablespoons lemon juice
¼ teaspoon jalapeño relish
1 teaspoon salt
1½ cups puréed ripe avocado
Green food coloring

Soften gelatin in ¼ cup cold water. Add ¼ cup boiling water. Stir in lemon juice, jalapeño relish and salt. Cool until thick. Stir in avocado and add a little green food coloring. Pour into 9x5x2½" loaf pan. Chill until almost firm. While this is setting, prepare the cheese layer.

Cheese Layer:

2 teaspoons gelatine
½ cup milk
12 oz. cream cheese
1 teaspoon salt
1 tablespoon grated onion
⅔ cup mayonnaise
Dash of HOT pepper sauce
¼ teaspoon Worcestershire
    sauce

Soften gelatine in ¼ cup cold water. Dissolve over boiling water. Gradually mix milk with cream cheese until well combined. Blend in other ingredients. Stir in dissolved gelatine. Spread over avocado layer. Chill.

Tomato Layer:

3 cups Bloody Mary mix
2 teaspoons dill weed
3 sprigs parsley
2 stalks celery
Salt to taste
Dash red pepper
1½ envelopes gelatine
1½ tablespoons lemon juice
1½ teaspoons grated onion

Simmer Bloody Mary mix with dill (use fresh dill if available), parsley, celery, salt and red pepper for 10 minutes. Strain. Soften gelatine with ⅓ cup cold water, add to hot mixture and stir until dissolved. Add lemon juice and onion, stir. Chill until partially thickened and pour over cheese layer after it is firm. Chill overnight, unmold and slice. Serves 8.

P.S. This is a beautiful salad and good too. It sounds like a lot of trouble but sometimes it's worth it.

P.P.S. I oil the inside of the loaf pan with a little mayonnaise to make it easier to unmold.

Potato Salad, Alberta

5 lbs. potatoes
10 eggs, hard boiled
6 stalks celery, chopped
1 bell pepper, chopped
1 onion, minced
½ bunch green onions,
    chopped
4 sweet pickles, chopped
2 dill pickles, chopped
12 stuffed olives, chopped
1½ to 2 cups mayonnaise
1 tablespoon prepared
    mustard
½ teaspoon paprika
Salt and pepper to taste

Boil potatoes in jackets, cool, peel and cube. Chop eggs. Combine all ingredients. Refrigerate overnight. Sprinkle with paprika and garnish with bell pepper rings.

Easy Tomato Aspic

8 artichoke hearts, canned
Italian dressing
1 tablespoon plus 1 teaspoon
    unflavored gelatine
1 cup vegetable juice
1 cup Bloody Mary mix
1 tablespoon lemon juice
½ teaspoon sugar

Drain artichoke hearts and marinate in Italian dressing for several hours. Drain artichokes on paper towels. Soak gelatine in ½ cup vegetable juice. Heat the remaining vegetable juice to boiling and dissolve the gelatine in it. Mix gelatine with the Bloody Mary mix, lemon juice and sugar. Rinse individual gelatine molds and fill ¼ full of juice mixture. Put in ice box until sets up. Put 1 artichoke heart in center of each mold and fill with remaining juice. Chill. Serves 8.

P.S. This is very good and it's much easier than boiling the onion, celery, etc. Use your favorite Italian dressing.

43

Pepper Steak Salad

3 cups thin strips of rare roast beef
1 large bell pepper (cut in strips)
1 cup sliced celery
⅓ cup chopped green onion
⅓ cup sliced mushrooms
½ cup teriyaki sauce
⅓ cup dry sherry
3 tablespoons white vinegar
⅓ cup salad oil
½ teaspoon ground ginger
2 small tomatoes (cut in wedges)
1 cup fresh bean sprouts
3 cups shredded Chinese cabbage

Combine beef, pepper, celery, onion and mushrooms. Combine teriyaki sauce, sherry, vinegar, oil and ginger and blend thoroughly. Pour over beef mixture. Toss well. Cover and refrigerate 2 or 3 hours. Add tomatoes and bean sprouts and toss again. Drain, reserving marinade. Place shredded cabbage in large salad bowl. Cover with marinated meat and vegetables. Serve reserved marinade for dressing. Serves 6-8.

P.S. Try this some hot night with French bread. Serve with cold fresh fruit and you have a "super" supper.

Sauce Alexandre

4 tablespoons butter
4 tablespoons flour
1 cup chicken broth
Salt and pepper to taste
½ lb. fresh mushrooms
1 tablespoon finely chopped green onion
¼ cup dry white wine
1½ cups heavy cream

Melt 3 tablespoons butter in a saucepan and add flour, stirring with wire whisk. When smooth, add chicken broth and continue to stir. Season with salt and pepper and simmer about 10 minutes, stirring occasionally. Slice mushrooms thin. Melt the remaining tablespoon of butter in a pan and add mushrooms. Season with salt and pepper and sauté until mushrooms are done. Add onions and stir, continuing to cook until most of the liquid has evaporated. Add wine and cook until wine is reduced to one half. Add the butter and flour mixture and the cream. Bring to a boil, stirring well.

P.S. This is a very versatile sauce. Good over an omelet, vegetables, meat loaf and many other things.

Barbecue Sauce

½ cup burgundy
½ cup chili sauce
¼ cup salad oil
3 tablespoons wine vinegar
2 cloves garlic
3 tablespoons finely chopped onion
3 tablespoons Worcestershire sauce
1 bay leaf
Salt and pepper (to taste)

Combine all ingredients and pour over meat. Marinate (turning meat occasionally) from 3 hours to 3 days in covered bowl or in plastic bag which has been securely tied.

P.S. Everbody has a favorite barbecue sauce. This is mine. Try it with thick pork chops.

Avocado Mushroom Sauce

½ cup chopped fresh
  mushrooms
1 tablespoon finely chopped
  onion
2 tablespoons butter
2 tablespoons flour
½ teaspoon salt
1 cup milk
½ cup sour cream
1 ripe avocado, mashed

In medium saucepan, cook mushrooms and onion in butter until the onion is tender, but not brown. Stir in flour and salt. Add milk all at once. Cook over medium heat, stirring constantly until thickened. Remove from heat, stir in sour cream and avocado. Heat.

P.S. You can serve this as a dip for shrimp or raw vegetables, or as a hot dip with corn chips. It's good over omelets, sliced ham or anything you dream up. I think its really good!

Chasseur Sauce

¼ lb. mushrooms, chopped
1 green onion, finely chopped
4 tablespoons butter
1 (¾ oz.) envelope brown
  gravy mix
¾ cup water
¼ cup dry red wine
1 tablespoon tomato paste
½ teaspoon mixed herbs

In 1½ quart saucepan, sauté mushrooms and onion in butter until tender, but not brown. Blend in brown gravy mix. Add water, wine, tomato paste and herbs. Cook over medium heat, stirring constantly until thickened.

P.S. This is very easy and tasty. Serve over sliced beef, meat balls, chicken or turkey. It will help almost any left over.

P.P.S. I like basil, thyme and rosemary for my herbs, but use the ones you like.

Béarnaise Sauce

1 lb. butter (1½ cups clarified)
2 tablespoons finely chopped
green peppers
2 tablespoons white wine
vinegar
1 teaspoon peppercorns,
crushed
1 tablespoon dried tarragon
2 egg yolks
2 tablespoons water
Salt to taste
Dash red pepper

Clarify the butter by melting it slowly and pouring it off, leaving the clear yellow liquid at the bottom of the saucepan. There should be about 1½ cups of clarified butter.

In a small saucepan (do not use aluminum), put peppercorns, onions, tarragon and vinegar. Bring to a boil and simmer until vinegar evaporates. Remove from heat. Add egg yolks and water and beat well with wire whisk. Put over low heat and continue beating until mixture thickens. Gradually add clarified butter and beat mixture until it reaches the consistency of mayonnaise. Add salt and red pepper.

P.S. You can keep this in the refrigerator, but when you reheat it, stir gently and do not get it too hot or it will separate. Makes about 1½ cups.

Celery Seed Honey Dressing

½ cup sugar
1 teaspoon dry mustard
1 teaspoon paprika
¼ teaspoon salt
1 tablespoon celery seed
⅓ cup honey
1 tablespoon lemon juice
4 tablespoons vinegar
1 teaspoon grated onion
1 cup salad oil

Mix dry ingredients, add honey, lemon juice, vinegar and onion. Pour in the oil and beat well. Serve with fruit salad.

P.S. Keeps indefinitely in the refrigerator in a closed jar.

Curried Vegetable Sauce

½ cup finely chopped onion
½ cup finely chopped green
  pepper
2 tablespoons margarine
1 tablespoon flour
1 to 2 teaspoons curry powder
¼ teaspoon salt
½ cup milk
1 teaspoon chicken bouillon
  granules or 1 chicken
  bouillon cube
½ teaspoon Worcestershire
  sauce
2 tablespoons pimiento
  (optional)

In 1½ quart saucepan, cook onion and green pepper until tender, but not brown. Stir in flour, curry powder and salt. Add milk, ½ cup water, chicken bouillon granules (or cube) and Worcestershire. Cook, stirring constantly until thickened.

P.S. We think this is delicious over broccoli, asparagus, green beans, cauliflower or what have you. Add curry powder to taste. One teaspoon is enough for me!

French Dressing À La Marion

1½ cups salad oil
½ cup lemon juice
8 (3″) squeezes anchovy paste
6 garlic cloves, pressed
½ teaspoon salt
⅓ teaspoon pepper
7 dashes curry powder
7 teaspoons prepared mustard
16 dashes steak sauce
16 dashes Worcestershire
  sauce

Mix ingredients together and store in jar in refrigerator at least overnight. Will keep beautifully for weeks. Can be halved but need to keep same proportions of salt and pepper.

When using one half of an avacado, leave the seed in the other half — Refrigerate and it will not turn dark —

Toasted Coconut Custard Sauce

3 eggs, beaten
¼ cup sugar
Dash of salt
2 cups milk
1 teaspoon vanilla
½ teaspoon coconut
flavoring
½ cup flaked coconut,
toasted

In heavy saucepan, blend beaten eggs, sugar and salt thoroughly. Gradually stir in milk. Cook over low heat, stirring constantly (about 15 minutes). Remove from heat and immediately set saucepan in larger pan of cold water. Continue to stir mixture for a minute or two. Stir in vanilla and coconut flavoring. Cool. Before serving, stir in toasted coconut. Serve over cake or fruit.

P.S. To toast coconut, place a thin layer in a pan and bake at 350° until brown. The coconut will be crunchy if you add it to the sauce just before serving. Watch coconut carefully while toasting! Will keep in ice box.

P.P.S. This will improve most any dessert and can make a simple dessert a gourmet dessert.

Sour Cream Dressing

1 cup sour cream
2 teaspoons salt
1½ teaspoons sugar
½ teaspoon paprika
¼ cup white wine
¼ teaspoon white pepper

Mix together well. Store in ice box. This is a good dressing for making cole slaw.

French Onion Sauce

2 large onions, thinly sliced
  (about three cups)
3 tablespoons butter or
  margarine
2 tablespoons cornstarch
1 cup beef broth
¼ teaspoon Worcestershire
  sauce
2 tablespoons grated
  Parmesan cheese

In 2 quart saucepan, cook onions in butter or margarine until lightly browned. Stir in the cornstarch. Add beef broth and Worcestershire all at once. Cook over medium heat, stirring until thickened and bubbly. Stir in cheese.

P.S. A variation of French Onion Soup. Try with beef main dishes such as meat loaf or minute steaks. Peps things up, believe me!

Fruit Royale Sauce

1 (16 oz.) can of pear halves
½ cup strawberry jelly
½ teaspoon ground nutmeg
1 (11 oz.) can mandarin orange
  sections
2 tablespoon lemon juice
4 teaspoons cornstarch
¼ cup brandy

Drain pears, reserving ½ cup of the syrup. Slice pears and set aside. Combine the reserved pear syrup, strawberry jelly, lemon juice, cornstarch and nutmeg in the blazer pan of a chafing dish, stirring constantly until thickened. Place blazer pan over chafing dish burner. Add pears and oranges to sauce, let simmer for 5 minutes, basting fruit. Remove from heat. Pour brandy in ladle, warm over burner. Flame and pour over fruit. Serve fruit and sauce over ice cream, sherbet, gingerbread or cake.

P.S. This is elegant, and your guests feel that you have really tried.

Fruit Sauce

4 eggs
1 cup sugar
½ teaspoon cornstarch
½ cup orange juice
½ cup lemon juice
1 cup cream, whipped

Beat eggs lightly and add sugar, cornstarch and fruit juices. Cook in double boiler until thick. When cool, fold in whipped cream.

P.S. This is a good sauce over left over dry cake.

Garlic Marinade

1 cup vinegar
½ cup salad oil
½ teaspoon salt
2 teaspoons garlic salt
1 teaspoon celery salt

Beat or shake all ingredients well. Marinate meat for at least six hours. Drain well ½ hour before cooking.

P.S. Particularly good for pork chops that are to be charcoal broiled.

P.P.S. Increase salt if fresh garlic is used.

Golden Dressing

2 eggs
½ cup sugar
¼ cup orange juice
½ cup pineapple juice
¼ cup lemon juice
½ cup cream, whipped

Beat eggs, adding sugar. Add eggs to fruit juices. Put in top of double boiler and cook, stirring constantly, until thick. Cool and add whipped cream.

Note: This is delicious with any kind of fruit salad, and honestly, it is better than "bought" dressings.

Hard Sauce

¼ cup butter
¾ cup sugar
1 teaspoon vanilla
2 tablespoons brandy

Cream butter with sugar. Add vanilla and brandy and cream well. Serve with cherry tarts or any hot pudding.

Note: I think you would have eaten sawdust with hard sauce on it when you were young. The secret here is to cream, cream, and cream again until it is light and fluffy and the sugar is melted. You can cut the vanilla and add to the brandy, of course!

Hollandaise Sauce

4 egg yolks
½ cup butter
¼ cup lemon juice
¼ teaspoon salt
Dash of red pepper

Beat egg yolks until very thick. Melt the butter in top of double boiler, remove from heat. Cool, add egg yolks all at once, and stir hard. Add lemon juice, salt and red pepper. Place over low heat and stir constantly until sauce is the consistency of whipped cream. Serve warm over asparagus, green beans, etc.

Note: This is as near foolproof as any recipe for Hollandaise that I have ever tried. It will keep in the refrigerator and is good cold, also.

If your Hollandaise sauce curdles, add a spoonful of boiling water and beat hard with a wire whisk.

Blender Hollandaise

3 egg yolks
3 oz. cream cheese
½ cup butter
3 tablespoons lemon juice
1 teaspoon salt
Dash of red pepper

Put egg yolks and cream cheese in blender. Cover and blend until smooth. Melt the butter, add lemon juice and let it come to a boil. With blender on medium setting, slowly add lemon butter to the mixture in the blender. Season with salt and red pepper. When fluffy, put in top of double boiler over hot (not boiling) water. Keep sauce warm until you serve it. Serve with a sprig of fresh dill, if you can find it.

P.S. You say you can't count on your Hollandaise? This is foolproof and almost as good as the regular Hollandaise (but not quite).

P.P.S. This is a good recipe if you need to prepare Hollandaise in advance. It keeps well in the refrigerator and can be reheated easily over hot water, without separating.

Sauce Meunière

½ cup butter
1 tablespoon chopped parsley
1 tablespoon chopped green
  onions
½ teaspoon salt
2 tablespoons lemon juice
½ teaspoon pepper
1 teaspoon Worcestershire
Dash of HOT pepper sauce

Mix ingredients in saucepan. Stir over low heat and simmer a few minutes. Serve over fillets of sole or other fish.

P.S. Top with toasted slivered almonds for a change.

Orange Hollandaise Sauce

3 egg yolks
½ cup butter
2 teaspoons grated orange
    rind
½ teaspoon grated lemon rind
3 tablespoons fresh orange
    juice
2 tablespoons fresh lemon
    juice
HOT pepper sauce and salt to
    taste

Put egg yolks in blender or bowl of food processor. Blend for a few seconds. In saucepan, heat until almost boiling the butter, orange rind, grated lemon rind, orange juice and lemon juice, hot pepper sauce and salt. With blender or processor running at full speed, slowly pour in hot mixture. Blend until light and fluffy. Keep warm over warm, *not boiling* water.

P.S. If your sauce does not thicken, return it to saucepan and stir over low heat until thick. This is easy and good with almost any vegetable. The orange flavor is especially pleasant and different.

Kum Back Sauce

¼ cup vegetable oil
1 cup Lemon Mayonnaise
¼ cup chili sauce
¼ cup catsup
2 tablespoons water
Juice of grated onion
2 garlic cloves chopped fine
1 teaspoon prepared mustard
1 teaspoon Worcestershire
    sauce
1 teaspoon salt
1 teaspoon pepper
Dash paprika
Dash hot pepper sauce

Put all ingredients in quart jar and shake well. Keep in ice box. Makes one pint.

P.S. Delicious on shrimp or vegetable salad.

Lemon Mayonnaise

1 egg
1 teaspoon salt
¼ teaspoon white pepper
1 teaspoon dry mustard
¼ cup lemon juice
1½ cups salad oil

Put first 5 ingredients in blender or food processor and blend well. Add oil in thin stream while motor is running. If mayonnaise is too thick or does not accept the last of the oil, add a little more lemon juice.

P.S. This is a very useful mayonnaise. Using a whole egg instead of egg yolks makes it lighter.

If mayonnaise doesn't thicken, beat another egg and slowly add the thin mayonnaise —

Mint Patty Sauce

1 (3¾ oz.) package vanilla
   pudding
1½ cups milk
½ cup chocolate covered
   cream filled mint patties,
   cut in pieces
1 cup heavy cream, whipped

In 1½ quart saucepan, combine vanilla pudding mix, milk and cut up mint patties. Cook over medium heat, stirring constantly until thick and bubbly and mint patties are melted. Remove from heat. Cover with plastic wrap. Cool. Fold whipped cream into mixture. Cover and chill. When serving, cover sauce with chocolate curls and, if possible, a sprig of fresh mint.

P.S. Use to fill cream puffs, serve with chilled fruit or use as a frosting for angel food or sponge cake. Good!

My Sauce

½ pint strawberry preserves
2 tablespoons frozen orange
 juice concentrate
Juice of ½ lemon
1 teaspoon grated orange rind
1 teaspoon grated lemon rind
2 tablespoons sherry

Put strawberry preserves, orange juice, lemon juice, orange rind and lemon rind in saucepan and simmer until it begins to thicken. Remove from heat, stir in sherry and serve warm as sauce for custards, puddings or angel food cake.

P.S. Adds a lot to the finished product.

Basic White Sauce

2 tablespoons butter
2 tablespoons flour
¼ teaspoon salt
Pepper to taste
1 cup milk

Melt butter in small saucepan. Add flour mixed with seasonings and stir until blended. Use wire whisk to keep smooth. Pour in milk gradually and while stirring constantly, bring to boiling point and boil about 2 minutes.

P.S. If you want a thick sauce, use 4 tablespoons butter and 4 tablespoons flour. If you want a richer sauce, use part cream. Season with paprika, onion juice, onion salt, ¼ teaspoon dry mustard, or anything you desire.

Rémoulade Sauce

3 tablespoons wine vinegar
1 tablespoon Creole mustard
2 tablespoons minced onion
2 tablespoons finely chopped
  hard cooked eggs
2 tablespoons minced celery
1 teaspoon grated fresh
  horseradish
½ cup plus 1 tablespoon olive
  oil
Salt, pepper and red pepper

Combine vinegar, mustard, onion, celery, horseradish and egg. Beat in the oil a little at a time until thoroughly blended and creamy. Season to taste with salt, black pepper and red pepper.

P.S. Serve as a cocktail sauce for shrimp, crabmeat or what you like. Use Dijon if you can't find Creole mustard.

Vinaigrette Sauce

¾ cup olive oil
¼ cup lemon juice
½ teaspoon dry mustard
1 teaspoon finely chopped
  pickle
½ teaspoon chopped chives
1 tablespoon chopped capers
Salt and pepper to taste
1 teaspoon chopped parsley

Combine and chill.

P.S. Serve cold on vegetables or seafood, or heat and serve with hot boiled beef.

Russian Sauce

2 tablespoons butter
3 tablespoons flour
¼ teaspoon salt
Dash of white pepper
1 cup chicken broth
½ cup light cream
2 teaspoons chopped chives
1 teaspoon dry mustard
1 teaspoon prepared
   horseradish
1 teaspoon lemon juice

In small pan melt butter, blend in flour, salt and white pepper. Add chicken broth and cream all at once. Cook over medium heat, stirring constantly until the mixture thickens. Add chives, mustard, horseradish and lemon juice. Cook two minutes more.

Note: This is a glorified white sauce but it makes a gourmet dish out of baked or broiled fish and vegetables such as asparagus. Try it!

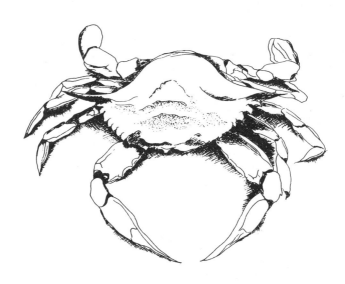

Breads

Brioche

1 lb. butter
2 tablespoons sugar
5 tablespoons milk
2 teaspoons salt
1½ packages yeast dissolved
  in ¼ cup warm water
6 eggs
4 cups flour

Dissolve yeast in warm water. Set aside. In large mixing bowl sift 4 cups flour, add sugar and salt that have been dissolved in milk. Mix well and add yeast solution. Beat 4 eggs and add to mix in bowl. With dough hook attached beat well. Then add other two eggs one at a time. Beat for about five minutes, until dough is smooth. Break butter into walnut size pieces and with mixer on low speed quickly add the butter. Cover bowl with a cloth and let rise at room temperature for 1 to 2½ hours (until doubled in bulk). Punch dough down and put on floured board and knead by hand for about 5 minutes. Put back in bowl and refrigerate. After about 3 hours in refrigerator punch dough down. Cover and let stay in refrigerator over night.

On a lightly floured table, break dough into about 16 equal pieces and roll each into a ball. Butter individual brioche molds and press ball into mold, filling mold about half full. Indent center and press very small balls of dough in center to form a "head."

Let rise about an hour and brush each brioche with a little beaten egg. Place in oven preheated to 450° and bake until brown.

P.S. These are very time consuming but well worth the effort. They freeze well. May also be baked in larger brioche mold, covered with fruit or sauce and used for dessert.

Banana Bread

1 cup sugar
¼ cup shortening
2 eggs, beaten
2 cups flour
1 teaspoon soda
½ teaspoon salt
3 tablespoons sour milk
3 mashed bananas
⅔ cup chopped walnuts

Cream sugar and shortening, add eggs. Sift dry ingredients together and add alternately with milk. Mix in bananas and walnuts and bake in greased loaf pan for 1 hour in 350° oven.

Note: If you like banana bread, you will like this. I don't!

Angel Biscuits

½ package yeast
1 tablespoon water
2½ cups flour
1½ teaspoons baking powder
1 tablespoon sugar
½ teaspoon salt
½ teaspoon soda
1 cup buttermilk
½ cup shortening

Dissolve yeast in water. Sift dry ingredients. Mix with yeast, buttermilk and shortening. Roll out to thickness of ½″ and cut with biscuit cutter. Bake at 350° until golden.

Note: You can bake as soon as you make, or you can put the dough in the icebox overnight. It will rise and taste like a cross between a biscuit and a roll.

Corn Bread

1 egg
¾ cup sour milk
1 cup self-rising corn meal
3 tablespoons melted
  shortening

Add well beaten egg to milk and add to meal. Beat well and add the melted shortening just before baking. Put in well greased muffin or bread stick pans and bake at 400° for about 20 minutes.

Note: This is our recipe for corn-sticks—no sugar, please!

Cheese Toast

1 cup sharp cheese, grated
1½ tablespoons milk,
  approximately
1 teaspoon mustard
1 teaspoon Worcestershire
  sauce
1 egg yolk, beaten
1 egg white
Bacon strips
6 slices thin bread

Mix the cheese with a little milk, to soften, and add mustard and Worcestershire. Add egg yolk to cheese mixture. Beat egg white very stiff and fold into cheese mixture. Brown bread on one side and spread cheese mixture on other side. Place a strip of bacon on top and put under broiler.

Note: This is good for Sunday night supper, when you are desperate!

French Raised Doughnuts

1 cup boiling water
¼ cup shortening
½ cup sugar
1 teaspoon salt
1 cup evaporated milk
1 package yeast
½ cup lukewarm water
2 eggs, well beaten
5 or 6 cups sifted flour
Melted butter
Powdered sugar

Pour boiling water over shortening, sugar and salt. Add milk and cool to lukewarm. Dissolve yeast in lukewarm water and stir into cooled mixture. Add beaten eggs. Stir in 4 cups flour and beat. Add enough additional flour to make soft dough. Brush with melted butter and cover bowl with damp cloth. Chill until ready to use. Roll dough to ⅛" thickness. Cut into 2½" squares and fry in hot fat (360°) until brown. Drain on paper towel. Sprinkle with powdered sugar.

P.S. This dough keeps several days in the refrigerator if covered with damp cloth.

P.P.S. Gigi introduced me to these. One bite and your diet goes out the window.

Croissants

1 yeast cake
2 cups flour
1½ tablespoons sugar
¾ cup milk (approximate)
Melted butter for glazing
¼ cup warm water
½ teaspoon salt
1 egg yolk
¾ cup butter

Soften yeast in water, add ½ cup of flour. Work to a paste and form a ball. Cover and let rise in a warm place for about an hour. Add salt, sugar and egg yolk then add remaining flour and milk alternately. Knead for about 5 minutes on a floured board. Cover and let rise for about an hour. Punch down and chill in refrigerator for about 30 minutes. Cut butter into slices. Put dough on floured board and roll into a rectangle ½" thick. Put butter on top ⅔ of dough. Fold to the middle the bottom third of dough and then fold over the top third to form envelope shape. Give dough one half turn and roll out into rectangle. Fold as before. Turn and roll again and fold. Put dough in refrigerator for 30 minutes and repeat the above process. Chill dough in refrigerator overnight.

Roll dough into rectangle about ⅛" thick. Cut in strips about 5" wide. Cut each strip into a 5 inch square and cut square into triangle. Roll the triangles beginning with wide end opposite the point.

Shape into crescents and put on baking sheet. Cover and let double in bulk. Brush with melted butter and bake in 400° oven until lightly brown.

I know Croissants are a lot of trouble, but if you find anything else this good that is easy —

Call me Collect!

P.S. This recipe makes about 12 large Croissants or 16 smaller ones. These must be made in a cool kitchen as the butter slices must remain firm. They freeze well.

Ruth's Cranberry Bread

1 cup fresh cranberries
1¼ cups sugar
3 cups flour
4½ teaspoons baking powder
1 teaspoon salt
1 cup milk
3 tablespoons melted butter
2 eggs, slightly beaten
3 tablespoons grated orange
   rind
½ cup chopped nuts

Grind the cranberries coarsely. Add to this ¼ cup sugar and set aside. Sift together 1 cup sugar, flour, baking powder and salt. Blend in milk, melted butter, eggs, orange rind and nuts. Fold in cranberry mixture and pour into greased loaf pan. Cook at 350° for one hour.

P.S. This will make 2 small loaves. Makes delicious sandwiches.

P.P.S. Cranberry bread always is a special holiday treat for my family.

Mamie's Dill Bread

1 package dry yeast
1 cup creamed cottage cheese
4 tablespoons butter
1 tablespoon sugar
1 teaspoon salt
¼ teaspoon soda
2 teaspoons dill seeds
1 egg
2½ cups flour (scant)

Dissolve yeast in ¼ cup warm water and set aside. Heat cottage cheese and butter in small saucepan. Pour into large mixing bowl and add sugar, salt, soda (dissolved in 1 teaspoon hot water), dill seed and egg. When lukewarm, add yeast mixture and flour. Beat on slow setting until well mixed. Cover and put in warm place and let rise until doubled in bulk (about 1 hour). Punch down and put in well buttered loaf pan, approximately 9x5x2″. Let rise again about 40 minutes. Bake at 350° for 40-50 minutes. Cover top with foil during last few minutes if necessary. Remove from oven, rub the top with butter and sprinkle lightly with salt. Cool in pan.

Henrietta's Rolls

2 cups milk
3 tablespoons sugar
½ cup shortening
1 tablespoon salt
2 cakes yeast
Flour, as needed

Scald milk, sugar and shortening together. Cool to lukewarm, add yeast (dissolved in ¼ cup cold water) and salt. Add flour to make soft dough. Let rise in warm place about 1 hour. Knead dough, roll and cut to make pocket book rolls. Let rise about ½ hour. Bake at 350°.

P.S. We cook them until almost brown, put them in bags and freeze them.

P.P.S. We think these are the best rolls we've ever tasted.

Ice Box Rolls

2 cups scalded milk
½ cup shortening
½ cup sugar (scant)
1 envelope yeast
4 cups flour
1 teaspoon baking powder
1 teaspoon salt
½ teaspoon soda

Scald milk, pour over shortening and sugar, cool and add yeast dissolved according to directions. Add about 1½ cups flour and beat well. Cover and place in a warm place until risen double in bulk. Punch down and add about 2½ cups additional flour with the baking powder, salt and soda. Knead and cover and put in ice box until desired. Make into rolls and let rise until very light and bake in about 400° oven until brown.

Note: This dough will keep in the ice box for about a week and you can use as desired.

Jeweled Christmas Tree
(for Christmas breakfast)

Basic Sweet Dough:

5-6 cups all purpose flour
2 packages dry yeast
1½ cups milk
½ cup butter
½ cup sugar
1½ teaspoons salt
2 eggs

In large mixing bowl, combine 2 cups flour and yeast. In a one quart pan, combine milk, butter, sugar and salt. Heat until warm and add to flour. Add eggs. Beat ½ minute at low speed, scraping bowl. Beat 3 minutes more at high speed. Add 1 cup flour and beat 1 minute more. Stir in enough flour to make soft dough. Turn onto lightly floured board and knead 5 minutes or until smooth. Place in buttered bowl, turning once to cover top. Cover bowl, let rise until doubled.

After dough has doubled in size, punch down and divide into 11 equal portions. Shape each portion into small balls. Place balls on buttered sheet in 4 rows. Form a tree by placing 1 ball at the top, then 2 balls below then 3, and then 4. Make tree base with final ball of dough. Cover and let rise until doubled, 25-30 minutes. Bake in preheated 350° oven until brown.

Glaze:

1½ cups powdered sugar
1½ teaspoons milk
½ teaspoon vanilla
Red and green candied cherries

Combine powdered sugar, milk and vanilla, spread glaze over tree and decorate with red and green cherries.

P.S. This is so pretty and so good for Christmas breakfast, and you can use your imagination in decorating. Bake the day before and reheat on Christmas morning.

Hush Puppies

2 cups corn meal
2 tablespoons flour
1 tablespoon baking powder
1 teaspoon salt
2 cups buttermilk
1 egg
6 teaspoons minced onion
(optional)

Mix well and fry in fat in which fish are fried.

P.S. We think fish caught at our own Windy Hill Lake are the best. Wherever you catch the fish, you can't beat these hush puppies!

P.P.S. Dad didn't like the onion in them.

Oatmeal Bread

1 cup quick oatmeal
½ cup vegetable oil
½ cup molasses
1½ cups boiling water
1 tablespoon salt
2 packages yeast
½ cup warm water
2 eggs
6-7 cups flour, approximately

Mix oatmeal, oil, molasses and add boiling water and salt. Soak yeast in warm water. Mix eggs with yeast. When the oatmeal mixture is lukewarm, add the yeast and eggs. Add to this enough flour to make a dough that is smooth and easy to knead. Knead and let rise until double in bulk. Shape and let rise again. Bake at 350° until brown.

P.S. I cook mine in buttered loaf pans. Makes 4 medium size loaves or 6 small ones. Easy and good.

Waffles

4 eggs
3 cups flour
4 teaspoons baking powder
½ teaspoon salt
2 cups milk
½ cup melted butter

Separate eggs, beat yolks well. Sift flour, baking powder and salt. To egg yolks, add alternately the sifted dry ingredients and the milk. Mix well, add melted butter, then add stiffly beaten egg whites. DO NOT BEAT.

Note: These are very light in texture. I know you can buy waffle mix but you can't buy any this good. Don't be so lazy!

Easy Waffles

1½ cups milk
¼ cup cooking oil
1 egg
1½ cups flour
3 teaspoons baking powder
1 teaspoon salt

Put all of the ingredients in blender and give them a whirl.

P.S. These are not quite as good as the first recipe for waffles, but what could be simpler?

Spoon Bread

1 cup corn meal
2 cups boiling water
1 cup sweet milk
¼ cup butter
2 eggs, well beaten
½ teaspoon salt

Scald the meal in the boiling water and allow to cool. Add the milk, butter, beaten eggs and salt. Bake in greased baking dish in moderate oven.

Note: We add the egg yolks first and fold in the beaten egg whites last. This is mighty fine with ham gravy!

Mother Walker's Potato Rolls

¼ cup milk
4 tablespoons shortening
¼ cup sugar (scant)
½ cup riced potatoes, hot
1 teaspoon salt
1 yeast cake
¼ cup lukewarm water
1 egg
1 egg yolk
2½ cups flour

Put milk, shortening and sugar in sauce pan and heat to scald. Take off heat and add hot riced potatoes and salt. Let cool to lukewarm and add yeast that has been dissolved in lukewarm water. Beat egg and egg yolk until well mixed and add to milk mixture. Stir in ½ cup flour. Cover and let rise in warm place until light. Beat in 2 cups flour and let rise again until about doubled in bulk. Turn onto floured board and roll to ¼″ thickness. Cut with biscuit cutter and fold into pocketbook shape, pressing edges down. Let rise again. Bake at 425° for 12 to 15 minutes, depending on size of rolls. Brush with butter while hot.

P.S. This was my husband's mother's recipe, and she was famous for her rolls. Mine were never as good, but I really tried! Got tired of, "They don't taste like mother's did!"

Sally Lunn

1 teaspoon sugar
1 package yeast
¼ cup water
1 cup milk
¾ cup shortening (½ butter
  and ½ vegetable shortening)
4 cups flour
6 tablespoons sugar
2 teaspoons salt
4 eggs
Melted butter

Dissolve yeast in water, add sugar and set aside. Scald milk and add shortening while hot. Sift flour, sugar and salt together. When milk mixture is lukewarm, add well beaten eggs, yeast mixture and flour. Beat well. Cover with cloth and put bowl in pan of hot water to rise. It takes about 3 hours for it to rise, beat dough down *several* times during rising period. Put in well buttered 10 inch tube pan. Let rise 1½ hours. Bake at 325° for 45 to 60 minutes.
Brush with melted butter.

P.S. This was in my mother's box of old recipes. She was not certain who had given it to her. Your Dad liked it sliced hot and served with lots of butter—and he never gained weight!

P.P.S. I bake mine in a Bundt pan and it looks like a big beautiful cake!

To test bread dough to see if it has risen enough, press finger into dough — if impression remains, dough is ready —

Swedish Bread

1 cup scalded milk
1 yeast cake
¼ cup lukewarm water
3½ cups all purpose flour,
    approximately
¼ cup melted butter
1 egg, well beaten
⅓ cup sugar
¼ teaspoon salt
½ teaspoon almond extract
1 egg yolk
Slivered almonds or sesame
    seed (optional)

Cool milk to lukewarm. Add yeast dissolved in water and ½ cup flour. Beat well, cover and let rise. Add 2 cups flour and beat and let rise again. Add butter, egg, sugar, almond extract and enough more flour to knead. Knead well and let rise. Shape into braids by dividing into 3 long thin ropes of uniform size. Braid these into a loaf. Place on a buttered cookie sheet, brush with egg yolk that has been slightly beaten with ½ teaspoon water. Let this rise. Sprinkle with slivered almonds or sesame seed and bake at 350° for about 20 minutes.

P.S. This is about the only home-made bread that I make, but we like this very much. I usually make 2 small loaves rather than one large one.

T.O.'s Popovers

1 cup sifted all purpose flour
¼ teaspoon salt
1 teaspoon sugar (optional)
1 tablespoon salad oil
1 cup milk
2 large eggs

Sift flour before measuring. Mix dry ingredients. Add oil, milk and eggs. Beat at medium high or by hand until smooth (about 1½ minutes). Fill greased baking cups or pans half full. Bake on center rack at 400° for about 40 minutes. Don't peek! If you have small muffin pans, reduce heat to 350°. Cook about 25 minutes.

P.S. Serve immediately with butter and jam or honey. Great as hot hors d'oeuvres for a small group 'cause "they'll eat 'em fast as you can get 'em out of the pan."

Cracked Wheat Bread

3 cups milk
2 teaspoon salt
¾ cup cracked wheat
¼ cup margarine
½ cup sugar
2 packages yeast
7 cups flour, approximately
1 egg yolk, for glaze

Combine milk, salt, cracked wheat, margarine and sugar in saucepan. Heat to boiling. Cool to lukewarm and add yeast which has been dissolved in ¼ cup warm water. Beat in flour. When dough can be handled, cover and let rise until double in bulk. Divide into 3 large or 4 small well greased loaf pans. Glaze with egg yolk beaten with 1 tablespoon water. Let rise again. Bake at 350° until brown.

Note: You need a very large bowl as this dough doubles in bulk when it has risen.

Meat,
Poultry and Seafood

Beef Burgundy

3 lbs. steak, cut into
  1" cubes
2 tablespoons flour
1 tablespoon salt
1 teaspoon pepper
½ cup melted butter
1 (10 oz.) can beef broth
2 cups burgundy
½ teaspoon thyme
½ teaspoon basil
2 (8 oz.) cans small white
  onions
¾ lb. fresh mushrooms

Dredge meat in flour, salt and pepper. Brown in the butter over moderately high heat. Put in large casserole. Add beef broth to pan, bring to boil, scraping up the browned bits that have stuck to the bottom and sides. Pour over the beef. Add burgundy, thyme and basil. Cover and bake in slow oven for 2 hours. Remove cover and add onions and mushrooms and cook 30 to 40 minutes longer. Gravy may be thickened with 2 teaspoons cornstarch. Serve over rice or noodles.

P.S. This is easy and very good. With a green salad, you have a complete meal!

Boeuf Au Fromage

1 lb. sirloin or filet mignon
½ cup flour seasoned with salt
  and pepper
2 tablespoons peanut oil
2 tablespoons butter
1 cup beef stock
1 tablespoon sour cream
2 tablespoons Roquefort
  dressing
2 tablespoons Parmesan
  cheese

Slice beef in 4 inch strips. Coat beef in flour. Heat oil and butter. Sauté beef, a few strips at a time. Pour beef stock and sour cream in skillet and mix well. Return beef to skillet and stir. Place in casserole dish and top with Roquefort dressing and Parmesan cheese. Place under broiler until slightly browned. Serves 4.

P.S. Serve with a baked potato and a green vegetable. If you think you don't like the Roquefort dressing, try it once. You can always leave it out the next time if you were right.

Beef Roast with Dill Pickle Sauce

4 lb. boneless rolled beef
  rump roast
1 clove garlic
¼ teaspoon ground ginger
Salt and pepper
2 tablespoons oil
2 medium onions, sliced
½ cup water
2 cups sliced fresh mushrooms
2 tablespoons chopped dill
  pickle
2 tablespoons chopped
  pimiento
1 tablespoon parsley flakes
1 teaspoon sugar
¾ teaspoon caraway seeds
⅛ teaspoon white pepper
2 tablespoons cornstarch
2 tablespoons pickle juice
⅓ cup sour cream

Rub the roast with garlic, ginger, salt and pepper. Discard the garlic. In a dutch oven, brown the meat on all sides in hot oil. Add onions and ½ cup water. Cover and simmer 2½ to 3 hours. Remove meat and onion to platter and keep warm.

Skim fat from drippings. Measure and add water to equal 1½ cups. Return broth to pan. Stir in mushrooms, pickle, pimiento, parsley, sugar, caraway seeds and white pepper. Blend cornstarch with pickle juice and 2 tablespoons water. Add to pan. Cook and stir until bubbly. Season to taste. Gradually blend 1½ cups hot mixture into the sour cream. Return sour cream to hot mixture and heat through. Serve over beef slices. Serves 8.

P.S. A good recipe for rolled roast!

Hamburgers de Luxe

1 lb. round steak, ground
¼ lb. ground veal
¼ lb. ground lamb
1 tablespoon onion juice
3 tablespoons cold water
1 egg
Salt and pepper

Cut off fat before grinding meat. Grind 3 times. Add onion juice, water, and egg. Salt and pepper to taste. Shape into hamburgers and charcoal broil.

Note: These are really de luxe. Try them sometime, they are best when served on rye buns.

Beef Wellington

3 lb. eye of round beef roast
4¾ oz. can liverwurst
1 egg

Marinade:

1 cup burgundy
1 cup dry sherry
1 onion, quartered
2 bay leaves

Combine marinade ingredients and marinate roast overnight. Remove roast from marinade, reserving ½ cup for sauce. Roast on rack at 350° for 1 hour and 15 minutes or until meat thermometer registers 130°. Reserve drippings and cool meat. Prepare pastry and roll out to 11x12″ rectangle. Spread liverwurst to within ½″ of sides. Place slightly salted and peppered meat topside down in center of pastry. Draw up long sides to overlap. Slightly beat egg, and brush pastry edges with egg to seal. Place on greased baking sheet, seam side down. Brush all over with remaining egg. Bake in 425° oven for 30 to 35 minutes. Serve with following sauce.

Pastry:

2 cups flour
⅔ cup shortening
½ teaspoon salt
⅓ to ½ cup cold water

Sift together flour and salt. Cut in shortening until mixture resembles coarse crumbs. Gradually add water, tossing until dampened. Roll into ball, cover with plastic wrap and chill.

Sauce:

1¼ cups water
3 tablespoons flour
Reserved marinade
Drippings
Burgundy
Salt and pepper to taste

Heat ¾ cup water with drippings until dissolved. Blend together flour and ½ cup water. Add to pan with reserved marinade. Add a little extra burgundy for flavor. Cook, stirring until thickened. Correct seasoning with salt and pepper.

P.S. This is an easier version of Beef Wellington and is very good. I frequently use my own recipe for pastry and season rather liberally.

Beef Strips in Red Wine With Mushrooms

2 sirloin or T-bone steaks
2 tablespoons butter
1 small onion, chopped
½ lb. mushrooms, sliced
1 teaspoon tomato paste
1 tablespoon flour
½ cup beef stock
½ cup red wine
Juice of ½ lemon
¼ teaspoon thyme
Chopped parsley

Remove bones from meat and cut meat in strips. Sauté the strips and mushrooms in foaming butter over high heat. Add onions and mushrooms and cook until onion is softened. Add tomato paste and flour and cook one minute. Stir with wire whisk until flour has absorbed butter and pan juices. Add beef stock and wine, stirring to form smooth paste. Flavor with lemon juice, thyme, salt and pepper. Cook 5 more minutes.

P.S. This is good served with noodles.

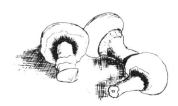

Oriental Casserole

1 lb. ground beef
1 medium sized onion, well
   chopped
1¼ cups uncooked rice
2 (10 oz.) cans beef bouillon
8 oz. fresh mushrooms,
   chopped
1 tablespoon Worcestershire
   sauce
1 teaspoon curry powder
Dash salt
Sour cream

Brown ground beef in *large* skillet and drain off excess fat. Add remainder of ingredients, except sour cream, and bring to a boil. Place this mixture in large casserole and cover. Bake at 350° for 1 hour. Garnish with sour cream.

P.S. It is the sour cream that "makes" this dish. Freezes well.

Steak in Phyllo

6 (8 oz.) beef filets, trimmed
   and salted
12 sheets phyllo dough
1 cup unsalted butter, melted
1½ cups filling

Cut 2 overlapping sheets of waxed paper a little larger than the sheets of phyllo. Butter a baking sheet. Put a sheet of waxed paper on baking sheet. Brush with butter, place a sheet of phyllo on paper. Add another sheet of phyllo and brush with butter. Place 1 beef filet 3 cm. from edge of phyllo. Spread steak with some of following filling. Fold 3″ flap of phyllo over steak, brush with butter. Using waxed paper, turn steak and phyllo over again. Brush with butter. Fold in long side of phyllo, and continue folding over steak, brushing with butter after each fold. Arrange seam side down on buttered baking dish. Repeat with other steaks. Bake at 350° until golden brown. Brush with butter twice during baking.

Filling:

¼ stick butter
2 tablespoons chopped onion
2 teaspoons minced shallots
2 cups finely chopped
   mushrooms
½ cup finely chopped ham
2 tablespoons tomato paste
¼ cup beef stock
¼ cup Marsala wine
1 tablespoon fresh lemon juice
Salt and pepper to taste

Melt butter in heavy skillet, add onion and shallots and cook until tender. Add mushrooms and cook 5 minutes. Add ham and tomato paste and cook 5 minutes more. Reduce heat to low. Add stock, wine, salt and pepper. Stirring constantly, cook until most of liquid is reduced.

Marinated Roast Lamb

Leg of lamb or shoulder roast, boned and tied

Cut slits in lamb and rub following marinade in. Place lamb in large plastic bag and pour in marinade. Seal bag and place in refrigerator for 12 hours, turning occasionally. After marinating, roast in roasting pan in 325° oven (3½ hours for 6 or 7 lb. roast). Use marinade with pan drippings for basting and gravy.

Marinade:

Combine all ingredients.

2 oz. olive oil
1 oz. lemon juice
1 medium onion, chopped
¼ cup parsley, chopped
1 teaspoon salt
1 teaspoon pepper
1 teaspoon marjoram
1 teaspoon thyme
1 teaspoon caraway seeds
2 garlic buds, minced
Slices of lemon that was
   juiced

P.S. If you don't have a fat separator, pour off liquid and place in freezer until you can remove grease, then warm it for making gravy.

"Leftover" Casserole

Slice (or if not sliceable, cut in strips) leftover beef roast. Put in bottom of casserole, add a layer of slices of raw potato. On top of this put several slices of onion and if you have any leftover mushrooms, add those. Take a pack of onion-mushroom soup mixed with ½ cup water and any leftover gravy you may have in the ice box. Pour over mixture in casserole and cook until potatoes are done.

P.S. When you live alone and meat is the price it is and your silly poodle won't eat beef, you think of lots of ways to use leftover roast. This is rather good.

Broiled Leg of Lamb

Have your butcher bone a 6 or 7 lb. leg of lamb. After it has been boned, with a sharp knife cut lengthwise through the thinnest part of the pocket and spread the leg flat. Peel off the parchment-like covering and slice away some of the fat under it. Prepare the following marinade and marinate lamb for 6 or 7 hours. Let lamb reach room temperature before broiling. Make your sauce while the lamb is marinating.

Marinade:

⅔ cup olive oil
1 teaspoon salt
2 tablespoons chopped
  parsley
3 crumbled bay leaves
1 cup thinly sliced onions
3 garlic cloves, sliced
3 tablespoons lemon juice
½ teaspoon ground pepper
1 teaspoon oregano

Mix all ingredients and put in large plastic bag with lamb. Secure top tightly and marinate 6 or 7 hours. Pre-heat broiler pan under oven broiler. Remove meat from marinade and without drying, lay fat side down on the hot rack of the broiler and sprinkle with 1 teaspoon coarse salt (may use table salt). Place meat on broiler pan about 4 inches from the heat and broil (without basting) about 15 minutes. Watch carefully, and turn heat down if meat shows signs of burning. Meat should cook until quite brown and even slightly charred. With a pair of tongs, turn meat over and broil other side about 12 minutes. (When you turn meat, brush with marinade and sprinkle other side with 1 teaspoon salt). When done, cut against grain in ¼" slices and place on warm platter, pouring any juice in broiler over it. Serve the sauce which follows separately.

Have roast at room temperature before cooking — Rub with oil before roasting —

Sauce for Broiled Lamb:

3 egg yolks
1 teaspoon arrowroot
  (or corn starch)
1 tablespoon lemon juice
1 cup chicken stock
1 tablespoon chopped parsley
⅛ teaspoon cayenne pepper
1 teaspoon salt

Put egg yolks, arrowroot, lemon juice, salt and pepper in top of double boiler. Beat with wire whisk, slowly stirring in chicken broth, and cook until mixture coats spoon. Keep warm in double boiler until ready to serve. Stir in parsley when ready to serve.

P.S. Bill gave me this recipe. Try it and you will always want to broil your lamb. After dinner, take a long ride on your bike!

Ham with Asparagus

1 lb. fresh asparagus
8 slices baked ham
4 hard boiled eggs, sliced
3 tablespoons fresh parsley
8 English muffin halves or
  rusks
Orange Hollandaise Sauce

Clean and trim asparagus. Steam until tender. Roll 5 or 6 asparagus spears in each slice of ham. Place on muffin half or rusk. Place 2 slices hard boiled egg on top of each and cover with Orange Hollandaise sauce. Sprinkle with chopped parsley.

Note: For this recipe, I get a small boneless ham and have it sliced thin.

To slice meat into thin strips, partially freeze and it will slice easily —

Roast Pork with Vegetables

3 lb. boneless pork roast
¼ cup oil
Juice of 1 lemon
1 bay leaf
1 teaspoon marjoram
½ teaspoon thyme
1 teaspoon sage
4 cloves garlic, unpeeled
2 cups stock (beef, chicken or both)
1 lb. parsnips
1 lb. turnips
1 lb. carrots
6 tablespoons butter
Salt and pepper to taste

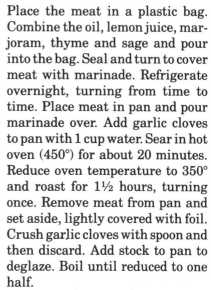

Place the meat in a plastic bag. Combine the oil, lemon juice, marjoram, thyme and sage and pour into the bag. Seal and turn to cover meat with marinade. Refrigerate overnight, turning from time to time. Place meat in pan and pour marinade over. Add garlic cloves to pan with 1 cup water. Sear in hot oven (450°) for about 20 minutes. Reduce oven temperature to 350° and roast for 1½ hours, turning once. Remove meat from pan and set aside, lightly covered with foil. Crush garlic cloves with spoon and then discard. Add stock to pan to deglaze. Boil until reduced to one half.

One hour before serving, pare and cut vegetables into 1″ pieces. Parboil in boiling salted water for about 5 minutes. Drain. Melt butter in a flat pan, big enough to hold vegetables in one layer without crowding. Coat the vegetables with the butter and place in 350° oven for 45 minutes. Turn vegetables during cooking to brown on all sides. Sprinkle with salt and pepper. To serve, surround sliced roast with vegetables, garnish platter and serve sauce separately.

Note: Of course you can roast potatoes this way but the parsnips and turnips make a nice change.

Mignonnettes of Veal Normandes

1 (½ lb.) round of veal,
  ⅜" thick
Flour for dusting veal
6 tablespoons butter (don't
  substitute margarine)
½ lb. fresh mushrooms, sliced
¼ cup apple brandy
¼ teaspoon salt
⅛ teaspoon white pepper
1 cup heavy cream

Preheat oven to 200°. Trim all fat and gristle from veal and cut into sections approximately 4" by 2". Pound until very thin to tenderize and dust with flour. In a large skillet, melt butter over low heat. Add pieces of veal and mushrooms, raise heat and sauté about 8 minutes until golden brown. Lift veal out, draining butter back into skillet. Place veal in 200° oven to keep warm. Add brandy to butter and mushrooms in skillet. Mix thoroughly. Add salt and pepper keeping heat low. Slowly pour in cream, stirring constantly. Raise heat to medium. When sauce thickens, reduce by ⅓ and simmer for about 6 minutes until sauce thickens slightly. Stir frequently. Just before serving, remove veal from oven and spoon sauce over portions.

Peggy's Chicken Artichoke Casserole

2 (14 oz.) cans artichoke hearts
2⅔ cups chopped cooked
  chicken
2 cups cream of chicken soup
1 cup mayonnaise
1 tablespoon lemon juice
½ teaspoon curry powder
Salt, pepper
1 cup bread crumbs
2 tablespoons melted butter
1¼ cups grated sharp
  Cheddar cheese

Grease 9x13" casserole. Drain artichokes well. Spread chicken and sliced artichoke hearts in casserole. Combine soup, mayonnaise, lemon juice and curry. Pour over chicken and season to taste. Mix bread crumbs with melted butter. Add cheese and sprinkle with bread crumbs over the top of casserole. Bake at 350° for 30 minutes. Serve over rice or noodles.

Chicken and Asparagus Casserole

2 whole chicken breasts
½ teaspoon salt
¼ teaspoon pepper
1 teaspoon monosodium
  glutamate
½ cup vegetable oil
2 (10 oz.) packages frozen
  asparagus or 1½ lb. fresh
2 tablespoons butter
3 tablespoons flour
¼ teaspoon salt
Dash pepper
⅛ teaspoon poultry seasoning
1¼ cups chicken broth
½ cup Lemon Mayonnaise
1½ tablespoons lemon juice
½ teaspoon curry powder
1 cup sharp cheese, grated

Skin and bone chicken and cut into 4″ pieces. Sprinkle MSG, salt and pepper over chicken. Pour oil into 10″ frying pan. Heat over medium heat, add chicken and sauté slowly about 6 minutes or until white and opaque. Remove chicken from pan, drain on paper towels. Cut frozen asparagus in half and cook by package directions. Drain. Place asparagus on bottom of 9x9x2″ casserole. Place sautéed chicken over asparagus.

Melt butter in small pan and blend in flour, salt, pepper and poultry seasoning. Add chicken broth and cook over medium heat, stirring constantly, until thickened. Add mayonnaise, lemon juice and curry powder and stir with wire whisk until blended. Pour sauce over chicken and asparagus, sprinkle with cheese. Bake in 375° oven about 30 minutes. Serves 4 - 6.

P.S. If fresh asparagus (which I prefer) is used, cut it into 3 - 4″ pieces and steam it until tender before making casserole.

P.P.S. If you want to, you can make a sauce in a hurry by adding 1 can cream of chicken soup to the mayonnaise, curry powder and lemon juice. It's good, but not as good.

Veal Scallopini

¼ cup butter
½ lb. mushrooms, sliced
1½ tablespoons lemon juice
¼ cup flour
1½ lb. veal, sliced very thin
1 teaspoon salt
¼ teaspoon pepper
¾ cup Marsala wine, dry
  sherry, or dry white wine
1 chicken bouillon cube
1 tablespoon minced parsley

Melt half of butter in skillet, add mushrooms, sprinkle with lemon juice and sauté until mushrooms are tender. Remove from pan and set aside.

Cut veal into 1" wide strips and dust in seasoned flour. Melt remaining butter and brown meat quickly on both sides. Pour in wine, add chicken bouillon cube dissolved in ½ cup water. Cook rapidly for a few minutes, stirring constantly. Return mushrooms to pan and heat. Serve at once, garnished with chopped parsley. Serves 4.

Chicken Austine

2 tablespoons butter
2 tablespoons flour
½ cup milk
2 cups diced cooked chicken
½ cup light cream
1 teaspoon salt
Dash of red pepper
½ teaspoon Worcestershire
  sauce
1 tablespoon sherry
3 avocados

Make a sauce with butter, flour and milk. Add chicken and cream and season with salt, red pepper and Worcestershire. Simmer for 3 minutes. Remove from fire and add sherry. Split avocados, peel and remove pits. Fill hollows with chicken mixture and brown under broiler.

Note: This is delicious and nice for a luncheon. It can be fixed in advance and heated at the last minute.

Saucy Chicken with Avocado

2 tablespoons butter or
  margarine
2½ to 3 lb. fryer, cut up
⅔ cup dry sherry
2 tablespoons flour
¾ teaspoon salt
Dash paprika
1¼ cups half and half cream
1 large avocado, peeled and
  sliced

In a 12″ skillet, melt butter. Cook chicken over medium heat until browned on all sides. Stir in sherry. Heat to boiling. Reduce heat to low, cover and simmer about 25 minutes. Keep liquid to about ½ cup, adding water and 1 teaspoon chicken bouillon granules, if necessary. Remove chicken to warm platter.

To liquid in skillet, stir flour, salt and paprika until well blended. Gradually stir in cream and cook, stirring constantly, until thickened. Gently add sliced avocado, heat through and spoon over chicken.

P.S. This may not sound good but I've learned to like cooked avocado and it is a little different.

Chicken Cacciatore

2½ to 3 lb. fryer, cut into
  quarters
3 tablespoons flour
¼ cup olive oil
2 garlic cloves, minced
1 (16 oz.) can tomatoes
1 large green pepper, chopped
1 cup chopped onion
¼ cup dry white wine
1 bay leaf
¾ teaspoon basil

On waxed paper, coat chicken with flour and salt. In 12″ skillet, brown chicken in oil over medium heat until all sides are brown. Pour off fat. Add tomatoes, juice and all. Add remaining ingredients and heat to boiling. Reduce heat, cover and cook 30 minutes until chicken is fork tender. Discard bay leaf. Serve with cooked spaghetti. Serves 4.

P.S. There are several versions of this recipe, but this is the one I like best. It's a nice change for the poor, overworked chicken dish.

Elegant Stuffed Chicken Breasts

6 boned chicken breast halves
Salt, pepper, seasoned salt
1 (3½ oz.) jar dried beef
3 slices bacon

Sprinkle chicken with salt, pepper and seasoned salt. Stuff breasts with 2 pieces of dried beef. Roll into mound. Place half slice of bacon over each roll. Pour sauce over chicken breasts and marinate 24 hours, covered tightly with tin foil.

Second day, cook at 350° until chicken is tender, approximately 2 hours. After first hour remove cover. Serves 6.

Sauce:

2 tablespoons butter
½ cup chopped mushrooms
6 tablespoons flour
1 cup chicken broth
2 tablespoons soy sauce
Dash white pepper
8 oz. sour cream

In small pan melt butter and sauté mushrooms. Remove mushrooms and reserve. Blend in 3 tablespoons flour. Add chicken broth all at once. Cook over medium heat, stirring constantly until mixture thickens. Mix 3 tablespoons flour with sour cream and add to sauce with mushrooms, soy sauce and pepper.

P.S. I add about 4 tablespoons red wine to the sauce. It makes the gravy look better and it adds to the taste.

When you boil a chicken for salad, or casserole, let chicken cool in the broth—will add to the flavor—

Chicken and Broccoli

3 whole chicken breasts
1 (10 oz.) package frozen
broccoli

Boil the chicken breasts. Bone and cut meat to make bite-sized pieces. Cook broccoli as per package directions. Line casserole with broccoli, then chicken. Cover with following sauce and sprinkle with ¼ cup grated sharp cheese. Heat until slightly brown on top. Serves 6-8.

Sauce:

2 tablespoons butter
3 tablespoons flour
¼ teaspoon salt
1¼ cups chicken broth
½ cup Lemon Mayonnaise
¾ cup grated sharp cheese
Juice of ½ lemon

In small pan, melt butter and blend in flour, salt and white pepper. Add chicken broth all at once. Cook over medium heat, stirring constantly until mixture thickens. Put mixture in double boiler and add ½ cup of cheese, mayonnaise and lemon juice. Stir with wire whisk until cheese is melted.

P.S. If you are in a rush, you can make a sauce by combining 2 cans of cream of chicken soup with the mayonnaise, lemon juice and cheese, but it's not as good.

Chicken Loaf

3 cups finely chopped chicken
1½ teaspoons salt
2 cups bread crumbs
1 cup cooked rice
⅛ cup pimiento, chopped
½ cup sliced, stuffed or ripe
   olives
4 eggs, well beaten

Mix all together, adding eggs last. Bake 1 hour in slow oven in greased loaf pan or ring mold. Serves 4 - 6.

P.S. I serve with Russian sauce in which I have substituted 1 teaspoon parsley for the horseradish. Heat sauce and pour over loaf when serving.

P.P.S If I am in a hurry, I make a sauce by mixing 1 can undiluted mushroom soup, ¼ cup butter, ⅛ teaspoon paprika, 1 teaspoon parsley, 1 teaspoon lemon juice and salt to taste. It's easier, but not as good.

Kauai Chicken

2 lbs. choice chicken
   pieces
1 teaspoon garlic salt
1 teaspoon paprika
½ teaspoon pepper
2 tablespoons vegetable oil
1 large onion, sliced
1 large green pepper, cut in
   thin strips
1 cup celery, diagonally sliced
1½ cups chicken broth
3 tablespoons cornstarch
3 tablespoons soy sauce
2 large tomatoes, cut in
   eighths
3 cups cooked rice

Remove skin and bones from chicken. Cut meat in thin strips. Season with garlic salt, paprika and pepper. Sauté chicken in oil until tender. Add onion, green pepper, celery and ½ cup broth. Blend remaining broth with cornstarch and soy sauce. Stir into chicken-vegetable mixture. Add tomatoes. Cook and stir until sauce thickens. Serve over rice. Serves 4.

P.S. You can prepare all the ingredients for this in the morning or the night before, and the cooking time is very short. The chicken is tender and the vegetables still nice and crisp. Makes it rather interesting!

Chicken Breasts À La Nancy

6 chicken breasts
2 tablespoons flour
Salt and pepper to taste
6 strips bacon
¼ cup butter
3 tablespoons sherry
1 cup diced cooked ham
1 cup diced cooked potatoes
1 (4 oz.) can button
  mushrooms
1 cup canned small onions
Hollandaise Sauce

Place chicken breasts in large roaster. Rub breasts with a little flour, salt and pepper. Cover each one with a strip of bacon. Cover the bottom of roaster with water, cover and steam in oven. When they have started cooking, add the butter. Baste very often, adding water as necessary to have several cups of stock. It takes a good while for these to steam tender. When almost tender, add sherry and continue basting. When breasts are tender, add the ham, potatoes, onions and mushrooms to stock in roaster. Let this heat well and then serve the chicken, adding around each breast some of the other ingredients. Cover with Hollandaise Sauce and garnish with fresh parsley. Serves 6.

Note: This is a whole meal and always makes a hit when I serve it.

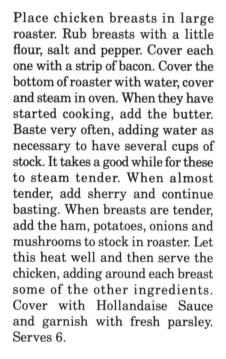

Increase your quanity of gravy by using chicken, or bouillon, cubes dissolved in water —

Chicken Casserole

2 tablespoons olive oil
½ cup chopped onion
¼ cup chopped green pepper
1 clove garlic, minced
1 (11 oz.) can tomatoes
1 (4½ oz.) can ripe olives, pitted
¼ lb. mushrooms, chopped
1 teaspoon sweet basil
1 teaspoon salt
1 teaspoon pepper
4 cups cooked, chopped chicken
1 (8 oz.) package noodles
2 cups chicken broth
Bread crumbs
Parmesan cheese

Brown the onion, green pepper and garlic in the olive oil. When brown, add the tomatoes, olives, mushrooms, basil, salt, and pepper and simmer about 15 minutes.

Meanwhile, cook the noodles in the chicken broth. Drain. Mix the noodles, sauce and chicken in a casserole that has been buttered. Bake at 350° for about 25 minutes or until brown. Serves 8.

P.S. I put buttered bread crumbs and Parmesan cheese on top, or 1 cup rolled potato chips.

Oven Baked Chicken Marsala

½ cup flour
½ teaspoon salt
1 egg
¼ cup milk
1 (2½ or 3 lb.) chicken, cut into pieces
1½ cups Italian style bread crumbs
½ cup Marsala wine

Mix flour and salt. Beat egg and add milk. Coat chicken pieces with flour, dip into egg mixture and roll in bread crumbs, pressing down firmly. Put breaded chicken pieces into well greased baking pan. Pieces should not touch. Dot with butter and bake in 350° oven about 45 minutes or until nicely browned. Do not turn. Drain off fat. Pour wine over chicken, cover with foil and bake another 5 or 10 minutes.

P.S. You can do this with sherry, but Marsala is better!

Chicken Divan

4 bunches cooked broccoli
Sliced boiled chicken
½ cup melted butter
½ cup flour
2 cups scalded milk
1 cup heavy cream, whipped
½ teaspoon Worcestershire
  sauce
1½ tablespoons Parmesan
  cheese
1 jigger sherry
½ cup Hollandaise Sauce
Salt and pepper to taste

Arrange a layer of broccoli in casserole and cover with sliced chicken. Combine butter, flour and milk in a saucepan over low heat and stir until thickened. Add cream, Worcestershire, wine and cheese. Mix until blended. Add Hollandaise. Season to taste. Pour over chicken slices and broccoli. Sprinkle with more Parmesan and brown under broiler.

P.S. This serves about 10 and is a good casserole. Couldn't write a cookbook without chicken!

Chicken in Hoisin Sauce

2 chicken breasts
2 teaspoons cornstarch
2 tablespoons sherry
8 water chestnuts
½ lb. fresh mushrooms
½ cup bamboo shoots
2 tablespoons peanut oil
¾ cup almonds, toasted
2 tablespoons Hoisin sauce
  (may substitute soy sauce)

Remove skin from chicken and cut into 1" cubes. Dissolve cornstarch in sherry. Marinate chicken in sherry and cornstarch for about 30 minutes.

Dice water chestnuts. Sauté mushrooms for a few minutes. Cut bamboo shoots in 1" pieces. Heat peanut oil in wok or skillet, add chicken, stir 2 minutes or until chicken turns white. Stirring continuously, add other ingredients and stir another minute. Serve with rice.

P.S. Such a quick dish to fix. If you can't find Hoisin sauce, use soy sauce. Not as good, but better than nothing.

Chicken Curry

⅓ cup minced onion
1 cup pared, cored and diced
   apples
3 tablespoons margarine
3 tablespoons flour
¾ teaspoon salt
Dash pepper
1½ teaspoons curry powder
¾ cup light cream
¾ cup chicken broth
1 lb. mushrooms, sliced
3 tablespoons salad oil
1 tablespoon lemon juice
3 cups cooked, boned chicken
¾ cup raw rice

Cook onions and apples in margarine in top of double boiler over boiling water until tender. Remove from heat and blend in flour and next three ingredients. Add cream and broth. Place over boiling water and cook, stirring until thickened. Cover, cook 10 minutes. Meanwhile cook rice. Sauté mushrooms 5 minutes in oil. Add to sauce with lemon juice and chicken. Serve with rice and with any or all of the following condiments: chopped peanuts, sliced eggs, chopped sweet pickle relish, coconut, raisins, scallions, fried onion rings, pineapple, mushrooms, fried bacon bits.

P.S. Serves many and freezes well.

Italian Chicken

6 thin slices boiled ham
3 large chicken breasts
1 medium tomato, seeded
   and chopped
½ teaspoon crushed sage
   (optional)
⅓ cup Italian bread crumbs
3 tablespoons grated
   Parmesan cheese
3 slices mozzarella cheese,
   halved
3 tablespoons chopped
   parsley
6 tablespoons melted butter

Skin, bone and halve the chicken breasts. Place chicken boned side up on cutting board. Place a piece of clear plastic wrap over it. Working from center, pound lightly with meat mallet until about 5x5 inches. Remove wrap. Place a ham slice and half slice of cheese on each cutlet. Top with some tomato and a dash of sage. Tuck in sides and roll up like a jelly roll, pressing to seal. Combine bread crumbs, Parmesan cheese and parsley. Dip chicken in melted butter then roll in crumbs. Bake in 325° oven until tender. Serves 6.

Chicken and Mushrooms in Wine

8 oz. Italian dressing
½ bottle dry white wine or
vermouth
1 pint sour cream
1 chicken, cut up for about
8 servings
½ pound fresh mushrooms,
whole
1 small package slivered
almonds

The day before you plan to serve this, mix together in shallow baking dish the dressing, wine and sour cream. Taste, add salt and pepper and more wine if needed. Put cut up chicken and raw mushrooms in marinade. Refrigerate until next day. About 2 hours before serving, set oven at 350°. Place pan uncovered on middle rack. Cover with sliced almonds. Bake 1½ hours. Taste again and correct seasoning. Serves 8.

P.S. I usually mix wine and vermouth about half and half. There are many ways to cook chicken, right?

P.P.S. I frequently add more mushrooms than the recipe calls for.

Chicken Chow Mein

1 medium hen
1 cup chopped celery
¾ cup chopped onion
½ cup chopped green pepper
(optional)
3 tablespoons soy sauce
Salt and pepper
1 (14 oz.) can mixed Chow
Mein vegetables
1 (8 oz.) can water chestnuts
½ (4 oz.) can bamboo sprouts
¼ lb. chopped mushrooms
1 tablespoon cornstarch
1 (3 oz.) can Chinese noodles
Toasted almonds

Boil hen until done. Remove bones and skin, and chop chicken in small pieces. Set aside, reserving broth. To the broth add celery, onion, green pepper (optional), and cook until tender. Season with soy sauce, salt and pepper. Add the remaining vegetables and the chicken. Cook until vegetables are tender, and simmer a few minutes more. Pour over heated noodles and cover with toasted almonds.

P.S. Add additional soy sauce to broth to taste. I usually add 1 tablespoon cornstarch during the last few minutes of cooking to thicken the liquid. This freezes well.

Chicken and Green Noodle Casserole

1 medium hen
1 cup celery, chopped
¾ lb. mushrooms, sliced
1 cup green pepper, chopped
1 onion, chopped
½ cup margarine
3 tablespoons flour
¼ teaspoon salt
Dash of pepper
¼ cup light cream
8 oz. Cheddar cheese, grated
2 oz. chopped stuffed olives
1 (7 oz.) package *green noodles*

Boil the hen, discard bone and skin, and chop chicken. Put chicken broth aside. Sauté the celery, mushrooms, green pepper and onion in the margarine until tender. Remove vegetables with slotted spoon. Add flour to drippings to make a roux. Whisk in about 1 cup of the reserved chicken broth and the cream. Season with salt and pepper and cook over medium heat, stirring constantly, until mixture thickens. Add sautéed vegetables, cheese and olives, and heat until cheese is melted.

Cook noodles in remaining chicken broth (add more water as necessary). Drain the noodles and pour into a buttered casserole. Add chopped chicken and sauce, and bake at 350° until browned slightly, approximately 30 minutes. Serves 8.

P.S. It is hard to find green noodles but you can.

Chicken Pot Pie

Pastry:

2 cups flour
4 tablespoons lard
8 tablespoons butter
2 or 3 tablespoons ice water
Salt

Filling:

5 tablespoons butter
2½ or 3 lb. chicken, cut into
  pieces
Salt and pepper
½ cup chopped carrots
½ cup chopped celery
1 cup small white onions,
  peeled
½ lb. fresh mushrooms, thinly
  sliced
3 sprigs chopped parsley
1 whole clove
½ teaspoon thyme
4 tablespoons flour
1 cup dry white wine
2 cups chicken broth
Few drops HOT pepper sauce
4 pieces bacon (cooked crisp)
3 hard boiled eggs
1 cup heavy cream
1 tablespoon cornstarch
1 teaspoon Worcestershire
  sauce
1 egg, beaten

Melt butter in skillet, add chicken sprinkled with salt and pepper. Cook about 5 minutes over low heat. Scatter carrots, celery and onions over chicken. Cook mushrooms until done in another pan. Add to chicken. Put cloves, parsley and thyme in cheesecloth bag, add to chicken and cook, stirring, for about 10 minutes. Sprinkle with flour, add wine and about 2 cups chicken broth. Add HOT pepper sauce, cover and simmer 30 minutes. Strain chicken mixture and put liquid in saucepan. Bone chicken and arrange with vegetables in baking dish (about 16x10x2″). Put crumbled bacon and hard boiled eggs, cut into 6ths over top. Skim fat from liquid in saucepan. Bring liquid to a boil and add cream. Simmer about 20 minutes (I add about 1 tablespoon cornstarch to thicken slightly). Add Worcestershire and correct seasoning to taste. Pour sauce over chicken mixture. Make pastry as you usually do. Roll out and arrange over chicken mixture. Brush with beaten egg and cook in 400° oven for 30 minutes. (Make a small hole in center for steam to escape).

P.S. A whole meal and very good, in fact, it is great!

Cornish Game Hens

2 Cornish game hens
Salt and pepper to taste
6 half slices of bacon
2 slices of bread
3 tablespoons butter
½ cup Cognac
½ cup cream
2 green onions, finely chopped
1 lb. seedless white grapes
½ cup port
1 tablespoon lemon juice
Red pepper to taste

Heat oven to 350°. Sprinkle hens with salt and pepper and place in well buttered roasting pan. Cover each hen with 3 half slices of bacon. Roast, basting with drippings, until tender. Trim the bread slices, cut diagonally and sauté in 2 tablespoons butter until brown. Drain on absorbent paper. Remove hens from oven, cut in half and place each half on triangle of bread. Keep warm. Put roasting pan over direct heat, add Cognac to liquid in pan and cook until reduced to half. Add cream and boil until creamy consistency. In small saucepan, heat 1 tablespoon butter, add the green onions and sauté 2 minutes. Add grapes and the port wine. Heat and ignite wine. Stir until flame is out. Strain cream gravy into grape sauce. Correct seasoning with salt, red pepper and lemon juice. Pour sauce over hens. Serves 4-6.

P.S. If fresh grapes are not available, you can substitute canned. If you don't think this is a fancy dish, try it!

Increase your quality of gravy by using chicken, or bouillon cubes dissolved in water—

Bob's Chicken Tetrazzini

4 or 5 lb. chicken
3 or 4 slices bacon
2 onions, chopped
2 green peppers, chopped
1 small bunch celery, chopped
½ lb. fresh mushrooms, sliced
1 (7 oz.) package spaghetti
1½ pts. Basic White Sauce
2 cups grated cheese

Boil chicken until tender. Remove bones and skin and chop up as for salad. Fry bacon, using grease to fry the onions, green pepper, celery and mushrooms until tender. Make medium thick white sauce and add cheese; cook spaghetti (do not overcook). Mix all ingredients, season to taste and pour into baking dish. Bake until brown. Serve 10-12.

Note: This is nice when you have company for it can be fixed in advance and heated up quickly.

Hot Chicken Salad

4 cups chopped chicken
2 cups chopped celery
½ cup Lemon Mayonnaise
2 tablespoons lemon juice
1 (10 oz.) can cream of
    mushroom soup
1 teaspoon chopped onion
2 pimientos, chopped fine
1 teaspoon salt
1 hard boiled egg, grated
1 cup sharp grated cheese
⅔ cup shredded almonds
1½ cups crushed potato chips

Mix, reserving ½ cup potato chips for top. Bake in buttered casserole at 350° for 20-30 minutes. Serves 8.

P.S. I add a little more lemon juice than the recipe calls for and a good dash of hot pepper sauce. Try this— you will like it!

Chicken Breasts with Sherry

6 chicken breasts (halves)
Salt and pepper
½ cup dry bread crumbs
½ cup Parmesan cheese
¼ cup cream sherry
½ cup margarine
Cooked broccoli

Bone the chicken breasts. Season with salt and pepper. Roll in the dry bread crumbs and Parmesan cheese. Place in pan with sherry and margarine. Bake 20 minutes at 350°. Baste with drippings and additional sherry. Cook covered with foil another hour, or until tender. Serve on broccoli stalks. Cover with following sauce. Serves 6.

Sauce:

2 tablespoons butter
3 tablespoons flour
Salt and pepper
1 cup chicken broth
2 tablespoons light cream
2 teaspoons chopped chives
4 tablespoons finely chopped
   celery
1 cup mild Cheddar cheese,
   grated
¼ cup sherry

In small pan, melt butter and sauté celery until soft. Remove celery and set aside. Blend in flour, salt and pepper. Add chicken broth and cream all at once. Cook over medium heat, stirring constantly until thickened. Add cheese and heat until melted. Add salt and pepper to taste, sherry and celery.

P.S. Good, try it! You also can make the sauce by adding the cheese and sherry to 1 can cream of celery soup. It!s easier, but not as good.

Chicken with Port Cream

4 chicken breasts (may use fryer, cut up)
3 tablespoons butter
½ cup port
¾ cup heavy cream
¼ teaspoon rosemary
¼ teaspoon basil
2 egg yolks

Remove skin from chicken and sprinkle pieces with salt. Melt butter in large frying pan. Brown chicken in butter. Add port and cream. Cover and simmer until tender (about 30 minutes). Lift chicken into serving dish. Boil juice until reduced to 1¼ cups, add rosemary and basil. Beat egg yolks until thick. Very slowly add hot liquid to egg yolks and stir constantly. Cook mixture until it thickens. *Do not boil.* Pour over chicken and garnish with chopped parsley.

P.S. You can cook chicken the day before serving. Reheat and make sauce. Be careful adding hot liquid to egg yolks or you will have scrambled eggs in chicken gravy!

P.P.S. I like to serve this with fried shoestring potatoes and asparagus.

When you boil a chicken for salad, or casserole, let chicken cool in the broth— Will add to the flavor—

Oriental Chicken Breasts

3 whole chicken breasts
1 (14 oz.) can Chinese
  vegetables, drained
8 oz. water chestnuts, sliced
½ cup chopped mushrooms
6 slices bacon
1½ tablespoons cornstarch
Chicken broth

Marinade:
½ cup vegetable oil
¼ cup lemon juice
¼ cup soy sauce
2 tablespoons finely chopped
  onion
¼ cup white wine
Salt and pepper to taste
1 teaspoon monosodium
  glutamate (optional)

Have your butcher slice through each side of the breasts to the bone, making a pocket in the breasts. Cut the breasts in half. Mix the Chinese vegetables, water chestnuts and mushrooms. Fill the pockets in the breasts with mixed vegetables, pulling the top over and securing with a tooth pick. Wrap a slice of bacon around each breast. Place in long casserole and cover with the marinade. Let marinate overnight. Place casserole (covered) in oven and cook until chicken is tender, basting often. Cook uncovered until lightly browned. If it cooks too dry, add chicken broth to liquid. Put chicken on a hot platter and keep warm. Skim fat from liquid in casserole. You should have about 1½ cups of liquid. Mix cornstarch with a little chicken broth. Add to liquid, correcting seasoning with additional soy sauce and wine if necessary. Cook until thickened. Serve with rice. Serves 6.

P.S. This is really delicious. Serve with green grape salad. Really a good meal!

P.P.S. I like to make this the day before I use it so that the fat can be skimmed easily. It reheats nicely.

Chicken Piquante

3 chickens (approximately
   3 lbs. each), boiled
12 tablespoons flour
12 tablespoons margarine
4 cups chopped green onion
2 cups chopped celery
4 cups chopped onions
6 cloves garlic, minced
4 (16 oz.) cans tomatoes
4 (8 oz.) cans tomato sauce
4 cups water
2 tablespoons salt
2 tablespoons monosodium
   glutamate
2 teaspoons black pepper
6 bay leaves
2 tablespoons Worcestershire
   sauce
2 teaspoons HOT pepper sauce
6 tablespoons sugar
4 tablespoons lemon juice
12 oz. claret or burgundy

Bone chickens and cut in bite sized pieces. In roasting pan, make a dark brown roux with the flour and margarine. Add green onion, celery, onions and garlic. Sauté for 10 minutes. Add the chicken and remaining ingredients. Bake at 350° for 2 hours.

P.S. This makes a turkey roaster full and serves 20 people. Can be divided into 4 casseroles. Freezes well.

P.P.S. You can use this same sauce with 5 pounds cubed pork or 5 pounds sliced cooked sausage—or a combination of chicken and pork.

Dell's Chicken Spaghetti

1 large hen
Salt and pepper
1 cup chopped onion
1 cup chopped green pepper
2 cups chopped celery
2 cloves garlic, minced
1 (11 oz.) can tomatoes
1 (7 oz.) package spaghetti
1 lb. sharp cheese, grated
6 oz. stuffed olives, sliced
½ lb. mushrooms
Grated Parmesan cheese

Boil hen and reserve all broth. Cool, bone and cut up chicken. To broth, add salt and pepper to taste, onion, green pepper, celery and garlic. Put tomatoes in blender and when blended, add to broth. Cook until vegetables are tender. Strain the broth, reserving the vegetables. Pour spaghetti in boiling broth and cook until tender. Drain spaghetti, reserving broth. Put spaghetti, vegetables, grated cheese, olives, mushrooms and chicken in casserole. Mix and add sufficient broth to moisten, heat in 325° oven for 20 minutes, cover with Parmesan cheese before serving.

P.S. I like to sprinkle a little garlic salt in the bottom of the casserole before filling. This makes several casseroles. It freezes well and we keep a casserole in the freezer and heat as needed. I like this recipe because it is not too highly seasoned or too rich.

Put a tablespoon of vegetable oil in the water when cooking spaghetti or noodles—

Tommy's Chicken

6 chicken breasts (halves)
Salt, pepper and paprika to
  taste
4 tablespoons butter
4 tablespoons olive oil
¼ teaspoon crumbled
  tarragon
¼ teaspoon rosemary
Juice of 2 lemons
1½ cups dry white wine
4 tablespoons sherry
4 tablespoons chicken stock
  base
1 lb. fresh mushrooms,
  sautéed
12 artichoke hearts

Season chicken breasts with salt, pepper and paprika. Lightly brown and place in roasting pan.

Put butter, olive oil, tarragon, rosemary, lemon juice, white wine, sherry and chicken stock base in saucepan and heat. Pour sauce over chicken breasts and cook slowly (300°) in oven until tender. Baste frequently. About 10 minutes before chicken is done, add mushrooms and artichoke hearts to sauce. Serve each chicken breast with mushrooms and two artichoke hearts. Serves 6.

P.S. Serve a mound of rice with sauce on each plate. You can make very attractive individual servings on each plate. Or arrange the chicken breasts with mushrooms and artichokes around a mound of rice on a platter. Garnish with something colorful like parsley and pimiento or wedges of tomato.

Baked Quail

8 quail
½ cup butter
2½ cups sliced mushrooms
¼ cup chopped green onions
1 cup white wine
2 tablespoons lemon juice
Salt and pepper to taste

Brown quail in butter. Remove quail and sauté mushrooms and onions in the butter. Place quail, mushrooms and onions in shallow pan and cover with foil. Bake at 350° for 1 hour. Baste often with combined juices. Remove foil during last 15 minutes of baking. Serve with wild rice.

Henrietta's Turkey Dressing
(For an average sized turkey (12-15 lbs.)

1 biscuit pan of cornbread
10 slices bread
3 eggs
1 onion, finely chopped
6 stalks celery, finely chopped
Turkey stock
Salt and pepper to taste

Break up cornbread and bread, mixing together. Add the onion and celery, which have been cooked in some of the turkey stock until tender, and the eggs. Season to taste and stir in enough of the turkey stock to make the right consistency (it should be moist). Stuff inside of turkey and cook for the last 30 minutes, or cook in casserole until lightly brown.

P.S. This was as near as Henrietta could come to giving this recipe, but I think you can make it. She says if you don't cook the onion and celery before you put it in the dressing, it won't taste good!

P.P.S. Henrietta also molds some of the uncooked dressing into small balls (about 1½ inches in diameter) and bakes them at 350° for 20 to 25 minutes until they are crisp on the outside. My children thought these "dressing cakes" were the best part of the turkey when they were young. They still like them!

Increase your quantity of gravy by using chicken, or bouillon cubes dissolved in water—

My Turkey Dressing

3 cups (approximately) crumbled corn bread
5 slices broken white bread
3 cups turkey stock
3 tablespoons finely chopped onion
5 tablespoons finely chopped celery
⅛ teaspoon rosemary
½ teaspoon basil
¼ cup dry white wine
Salt and pepper to taste
½ cup chopped mushrooms
½ cup thinly sliced water chestnuts

Mix corn bread and white bread. Put three cups of turkey stock in saucepan. Add onion, celery, rosemary and basil. Cook until onion and celery are tender. Add wine, salt and pepper to taste. Pour over cornbread mixture, mix lightly. It should be moist (add more stock if necessary). Add mushrooms and water chestnuts. Bake in buttered casserole until firm and slightly browned and serve with turkey and turkey gravy.

P.S. I made this up in desperation one Sunday when we were cooking a turkey on the barbecue spit and your Dad called for dressing in no uncertain terms! I happened to have some frozen turkey stock and the white wine was to stretch that. It was so successful that I have to make all the dressing now. You can use chicken bouillion cubes for added liquid, as needed.

*When buying fresh mushrooms.
the cap should be closed around the stem —*

Hot Turkey Soufflé

½ cup mushrooms, chopped
2 tablespoons butter
3 tablespoons flour
1½ cups chicken stock
6 slices white bread
2 cups chopped turkey
½ cup chopped green pepper
½ cup chopped celery
½ cup chopped onion
½ cup Lemon Mayonnaise
¾ teaspoon salt
2 eggs, beaten
1½ cups milk
½ cup sharp cheese, grated
Sliced almonds (optional)

Sauté mushrooms in melted butter. Add flour and stir until combined. Add chicken stock and cook over medium heat until sauce begins to thicken. Cut 2 slices of bread in cubes and place in the bottom of 2 quart casserole. Combine turkey, green pepper, celery, onion, mushroom sauce, mayonnaise and salt. Pour into casserole. Cube remaining slices of bread and place on top of casserole. Combine beaten eggs and milk and pour over mixture. Cover and chill overnight. Sprinkle with cheese and almonds and bake in slow oven for 1 hour or until set.

P.S. It's good to have something to do with that last 2 cups of turkey when you have been wondering why you bought such a big bird. This is really quite good.

Turkey Poulette

4 slices white bread, toasted
4 slices turkey breast
4 slices ham
1 (15 oz.) can asparagus spears
1½ cups Basic White Sauce
½ cup sharp cheese, grated

Melt cheese in white sauce and season well with salt, pepper and hot pepper sauce. Arrange toast slices on baking sheet, cover each with a slice of ham, asparagus spears, then a slice of turkey. Pour cheese sauce over each toast slice and run under broiler until bubbly and beginning to brown.

P.S. This is our favorite for the day after!

Barbecued Turkey

1 medium sized turkey

Barbecue sauce:
½ cup lemon juice
2 tablespoons Worcestershire
  sauce
4 tablespoons light brown
  sugar
1 teaspoon salt
¼ teaspoon garlic powder
¼ teaspoon dry mustard
¼ teaspoon paprika
½ cup butter, melted

Blend all ingredients, except butter. Use to marinate turkey for several hours or overnight. When ready to barbecue, remove bird from marinade. Melt butter, add remaining marinade. Place turkey in boat made from heavy duty aluminum foil. Brush marinade over turkey during barbecuing, liberally and frequently.

P.S. Longer marinating time intensifies barbecue flavor.

Mississippi Coast Gumbo

2 tablespoons fat or oil
2 tablespoons flour
3 cloves garlic, minced
2 tablespoons Worcestershire
  sauce
1 tablespoon parsley
4 sprigs thyme
4 bay leaves
½ teaspoon salt
½ teaspoon pepper
2 teaspoons monosodium
  glutamate
1 (16 oz.) can tomatoes
1 cup chicken broth
1 lb. shrimp
1 lb. fresh okra (or 14 oz. can)
½ lb. crab meat
2 large onions, minced
4 tablespoons chopped celery
Cooked rice

Place fat in large kettle, add flour and brown. Add all seasonings and tomatoes to browned flour. Add chicken broth and shrimp. Let cook until all seasonings are absorbed. Add liquid (water or stock) if too dry. Add okra, crabmeat, onion, and celery. (If fresh okra, add ½ hour before adding crabmeat.) Let simmer at least 1½ hours after adding crabmeat, stirring occasionally. When serving, place small amount of cooked rice in bowl and pour gumbo over. This makes 20 good sized cups.

P.S. If you have fresh lump crabmeat, I suggest you save some of it and when serving add a small amount to each cup of gumbo.

Shrimp Gumbo

1 small (2½ to 3 lb.) hen
1 cup chopped onion
1 cup chopped celery
½ cup chopped bell pepper
Chicken fat or vegetable oil
   for frying
2 (10 oz.) packages cut frozen
   okra or 2 (14 oz.) cans
6 oz. tomato paste
2 cloves of garlic
2 bay leaves
Salt and pepper to taste
3 lbs. shrimp, peeled and
   deveined
1 lb. of crab meat
1 pt. oysters
2½ tablespoons gumbo filé
Hot pepper sauce
Liquid crab boil

Boil hen until done. Save the broth. Remove chicken meat from bones, cut into small pieces and set aside. In large soup kettle or dutch oven, brown the onion, celery and bell pepper in chicken fat or oil. When brown, add okra and let it brown lightly. Add the tomato paste, then add chicken broth, garlic, and bay leaves. Season to taste with salt and pepper. Let simmer several hours, adding water when necessary and stirring often. When mixture has cooked to pieces, add shrimp, crab-meat, chicken pieces and oysters (with their liquid). A few minutes before serving add the gumbo filé and adjust seasoning with salt, pepper, hot pepper sauce and a couple of drops of liquid crab boil. Serve in a soup bowl with a spoonful of cooked rice in the center. Serves 10-12.

Note: This is expensive and somewhat troublesome, but is a whole meal. Serve it with salad and French bread and you have it made!

Batter for Frying Fish

⅓ cup flour
⅔ cup meal
1 beaten egg
1 can evaporated milk
4 or 5 dashes HOT pepper
   sauce
Salt

Mix flour and meal. Mix egg, milk, HOT pepper sauce and salt. Dip fish in egg mixture and then roll in flour and meal.

P.S. This recipe is used in the Cat-fish Capital of the World, Belzoni, Mississippi.

Kittie's Gumbo

½ cup margarine
4 tablespoons flour
5 large onions, chopped
4 stalks celery, chopped
2 (10 oz.) packages frozen okra
2 qts. chicken broth
2 (16 oz.) cans tomatoes
2 pods garlic
3 bay leaves
4 tablespoons crab boil
Salt and pepper
Hot pepper sauce
2 lbs. shrimp
1 lb. crabmeat
4 or 5 crab bodies, if
  obtainable
1 pint oysters
2 tablespoons gumbo filé
  (optional)

Make a very dark roux with margarine and flour. Set aside. In skillet brown onion, celery and okra. When brown, put roux, okra, onion and celery in large saucepan. Add chicken broth, tomatoes, garlic, and bay leaves. Add crab boil in cheese cloth bag. Cook for a couple of hours on low heat. Salt to taste and add black pepper and a dash of hot pepper sauce. After okra, onion, celery, and tomatoes have cooked to pieces, about 30 minutes before serving, add shrimp, crab meat and (if you have them) crab bodies. About 15 minutes before serving, add oysters and if you like it, add gumbo filé. Skim fat as needed, remove cheese cloth bag. Serve in a bowl over rice.

P.S. This gumbo recipe is a favorite with my family. I serve it with green salad and hot French bread.

Maryland Crab Cakes

1 cup Italian seasoned bread
  crumbs
1 large egg
¼ cup Lemon Mayonnaise,
  approximately
1 teaspoon Worcestershire
  sauce
1 teaspoon dry mustard
¼ teaspoon pepper
1 lb. fresh crab meat

Mix bread crumbs, egg, mayonnaise and seasonings. Add crab meat. Mix gently but thoroughly. Shape into cakes (about 6). Cook in frying pan in just enough fat to prevent sticking about 5 minutes on each side. Serves 4-6.

P.S. You can use canned crab meat but it is not as good. Serve with lemon wedges or tartar sauce.

Marge Roberts' Jambalaya

2 lbs. HOT hickory smoked
  sausage
2 frying chickens, cut up
Flour
Salt
Pepper
Garlic salt
4 large onions, chopped
2 bell peppers, chopped
2 garlic cloves, chopped
Hot pepper sauce
Worcestershire sauce
Soy sauce
3 cups rice, uncooked
1 lb. shrimp, cleaned

Cut sausage in pieces and brown in large heavy pan, soup kettle or Dutch oven. Remove sausage. Dip chicken in mixture of flour, salt, pepper and garlic salt. Brown chicken in kettle in which sausage was browned. Remove chicken and add onions, peppers and garlic. Sauté until onions are transparent. Return sausage and chicken to container. Season with Worcestershire sauce (quite a bit) soy sauce (quite a bit) and hot pepper sauce. Add water to bring total liquid to about 6 cups. Bring to a boil. Add rice and shrimp. Cover and again bring to a boil. Reduce heat and simmer 30 to 40 minutes. DO NOT UNCOVER. Remove from heat and allow to sit (covered) for 10 minutes. Serves 12.

P.S. The secret of this is to have HOT sausage, preferably Louisiana hot sausage. If you can't find it, use smoked sausage and 1 tablespoon crushed red pepper.

P.P.S. This is a full meal with or without a salad. It freezes well and is great to have on hand when you haven't planned ahead for dinner.

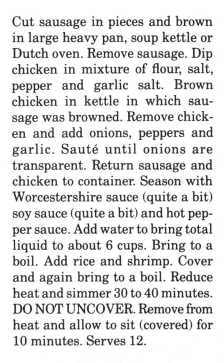

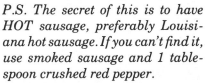

a pan of boiling water and vinegar on back burner will prevent fish odor —

Crabmeat Casanova

2 tablespoons butter
6 very thin slices lemon
2 teaspoons chopped chives
6 slices white bread, cut in
  rounds
1 pound lump crabmeat
2 teaspoons chopped parsley
5 tablespoons brandy
Salt and pepper to taste
Grated carrots for garnish

Melt butter in chafing dish or frying pan. Add lemon slices and 1 teaspoon of the chives. Sauté rounds of bread in seasoned butter until brown. Remove bread and keep warm. Add to the pan the crabmeat, the other teaspoon of chives, parsley, brandy, salt and pepper. Stir over burner until thoroughly heated. Pile crabmeat on sautéed bread rounds and serve with the grated carrots sprinkled on top.

Note: This is delicious. You will have to add to the melted butter as needed. Nice to make at the table in a chafing dish and **very good to eat!**

Scallops and Mushrooms

1 lb. scallops, fresh if
  available
1 teaspoon fresh lemon juice
1 small onion, chopped
2 tablespoons butter
1½ tablespoons flour
¼ teaspoon celery salt
¼ teaspoon thyme
½ teaspoon salt
1 teaspoon Worcestershire
  sauce
4 oz. fresh mushrooms,
  sautéed
1 jigger sherry
½ cup buttered bread crumbs

Wash and drain scallops and put in pan with lemon juice. Cover with water and boil about 3 minutes. Drain scallops, reserving about ¾ cup liquid. Sauté onions in butter, add flour and seasonings. Slowly add ¾ cup liquid and stir until smooth. Add mushrooms and sherry. Pour into baking dish, sprinkle with crumbs. Bake at 350° until brown.

Oysters Nancy

1 lb. fresh mushrooms, sliced
½ cup butter, melted
4 tablespoons lemon juice
1 tablespoon Worcestershire
  sauce
Small bunch green onions
2 pints fresh oysters, drained
½ cup half and half cream
2 tablespoons cornstarch
Salt and pepper
¼ teaspoon curry powder
2 teaspoons parsley flakes
5 tablespoons sherry
8 small puff pastries

Sauté mushrooms in butter, lemon juice and Worcestershire sauce. Remove mushrooms. Chop onions and heat in the skillet. When brown, add drained oysters. Stir and cook until oysters curl. Add cream to which cornstarch has been added. Season with salt and pepper, curry powder, parsley flakes and sherry. Mix mushrooms with oyster mixture and simmer until thickened. Pour into casserole and top with small puff pastries. Run in 350° oven 15 minutes to heat.

P.S. One Christmas I whipped this up in a hurry, had more people than pastries and had to improvise.

P.P.S. You may like to add more curry powder.

Seafood Casserole

4 slices bread
1 cup milk
4 hard cooked eggs, grated
1 medium onion, chopped fine
½ pint Lemon Mayonnaise
½ lb. crabmeat
½ lb. peeled shrimp
1 tablespoon Worcestershire
  sauce
Salt and pepper to taste
½ cup buttered bread crumbs

Soak bread in milk. Add all ingredients except bread crumbs. Mix well and pour into casserole. Cover with bread crumbs and bake at 350° for 45 minutes.

Hasty Seafood Casserole

1 cup chopped celery
¾ cup chopped onions
½ cup chopped bell pepper
2 (4½ oz.) cans shrimp
1 (7½ oz.) can crabmeat
½ cup mayonnaise
1 (10 oz.) can cream of celery
 soup
1 tablespoon lemon juice
Salt and pepper to taste
¾ cup buttered bread crumbs

Mix together all ingredients except bread crumbs. Place in casserole and cover with crumbs. Bake at 350° for 45 minutes.

P.S. You can put this together when you come home tired and have forgotten to plan ahead for dinner. With a green salad or green vegetable and French bread, you have a great dinner.

Broiled Scampi

1 lb. large shrimp
1 cup soft butter
4 green onions, finely chopped
4 garlic cloves, crushed
3 tablespoons bottled steak
 sauce or Worcestershire
2 tablespoons lemon juice
½ teaspoon salt
½ teaspoon freshly ground
 black pepper

Peel and devein the shrimp, leaving the tail attached. Split the shrimp lengthwise, being careful not to cut through, and spread them open. Put shrimp in an oiled shallow baking dish and broil for 5 minutes or until cooked through. Beat together or purée in a blender the butter, onions, garlic, steak sauce (or Worcestershire), lemon juice salt and pepper. Heat the seasoned butter until it is bubbling but not browned and pour over shrimp. Serves 4-6.

P.S. I like to leave my shrimp whole and turn them once during broiling as I think you get more of the shrimp flavor. So good!

Sole Meunière

6 fillets of sole
Milk
3 tablespoons seasoned flour
Peanut oil
3 tablespoons butter
1 tablespoon lemon juice
2 tablespoons finely chopped
  parsley
Parsley sprigs
Lemon slices

Divide sole down center line and discard bones, if any. Add enough milk to barely cover and let stand 15 minutes. Pat fillets dry and dredge in seasoned flour. Add oil to skillet to depth of ¼". When hot, cook fillets on both sides until golden brown. Remove from skillet and keep warm on serving platter. Discard oil in skillet and add butter. When it starts to brown, pour it over sole. Sprinkle with lemon juice and chopped parsley. Garnish platter with lemon slices and sprigs of parsley. Serves 6-8.

P.S. Cook any fish fillets in this way. Easy and good.

Sole with Shallots in Cream

½ cup minced shallots
¼ lb. fresh mushrooms, sliced
2 tablespoons minced parsley
1 lb. fillets of sole
½ cup dry white wine
Salt and pepper
1 cup heavy cream
Parsley for garnish
1 tomato

In a wide frying pan, spread shallots, mushrooms and parsley. Place sole fillets on top (overlapping as little as possible). Pour in wine. Cover and bring to a boil. Reduce heat and simmer 5 minutes. With wide spatula, transfer fillets to hot serving dish and keep warm. Add cream and seasonings to pan. Boil rapidly until sauce is reduced to about ¾ cup and takes on a pale golden color. When ready to serve, pour sauce over fish and garnish with parsley and tomato wedges.

P.S. If you cannot find fresh sole, this recipe is quite good with frozen fillets. Watch your sauce, for it scorches if cooked too long.

B.J.'s Barbecue Shrimp

1½ cups butter, melted
2 tablespoons salt
1 tablespoon thyme
2 lemons, sliced
1 tablespoon crab boil
3½ cups water
1 tablespoon black pepper
½ teaspoon garlic powder
4 tablespoons white wine
1 teaspoon seafood seasoning
2 lbs. raw shrimp

Mix sauce ingredients and bring to boil. Add shrimp and boil until shrimp are done. Serves 6-8.

P.S. I usually let my shrimp come to a good boil. Then I remove the pan from the heat and let it sit covered for about 15 minutes. Test your shrimp, for the size of the shrimp will determine the length of time they should stay in the sauce before serving. They are tough if cooked too long.

Shrimp and Chicken

¼ cup butter or margarine
1 cup chopped onion
1 small garlic clove, minced
3 whole chicken breasts, halved
2 teaspoons salt
½ teaspoon pepper
¼ cup port wine
1 (8 oz.) can tomato sauce
1 teaspoon basil
¼ cup finely chopped parsley
1 lb. shrimp, shelled and deveined (may use frozen shrimp)

In 12″ skillet over medium heat, put butter, onion and garlic and cook until tender. With slotted spoon remove mixture to bowl. Rub chicken breasts with salt and pepper. In butter remaining in skillet, cook chicken until golden on all sides. Stir in tomato sauce, wine, 3 tablespoons parsley and onion mixture. Heat to boiling. Reduce heat to low, cover and simmer about 10 minutes. Add shrimp, heat to boiling and simmer until shrimp is pink and tender. Sprinkle with remaining parsley before serving.

P.S. When I don't have enough chicken or enough shrimp for a meal, this is the way I combine them to have enough for all.

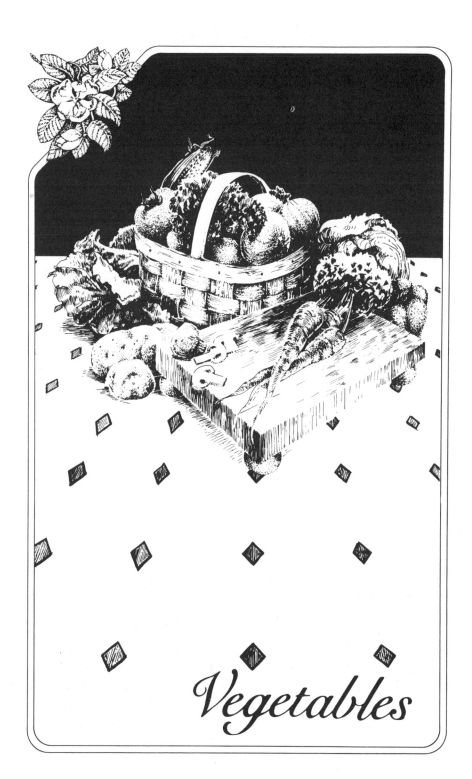

Vegetables

Asparagus Loaf

Large (15 oz.) can white
  asparagus
4 eggs, hard boiled and
  chopped fine
1½ cups Basic White Sauce
½ cup sharp cheese, grated
Buttered bread crumbs

Drain asparagus. Layer asparagus and chopped egg in 1 qt. casserole. Make a rich cheese sauce (Basic White Sauce that you melt sharp cheese in and season to taste). Pour sauce over eggs and asparagus. Cover with crumbs and bake in 350° oven for about 30 minutes until good and bubbly.

P.S. This was my mother's recipe.

P.P.S. White asparagus is sometimes hard to find. Green can be substituted although it is stronger in taste.

Asparagus and Shrimp Casserole

1½ cups mushrooms
2 tablespoons margarine
1½ cups Basic White Sauce
Salt
Pepper
Worcestershire sauce
1 tablespoon chopped parsley
2 large (15 oz.) cans asparagus
2 eggs, boiled and sliced
1 small can water chestnuts
1 small can ripe olives
½ lb. shrimp, boiled
1 cup grated cheese
Corn flake crumbs

Slice mushrooms and sauté in margarine. Add to white sauce and season with salt, pepper, 2 dashes Worcestershire sauce, and parsley flakes. Butter 1½ qt. casserole. Place layers of asparagus, eggs, olives, water chestnuts, mushrooms, shrimp and cheese in this order. Pour ½ sauce over this layer. Repeat layer, pour on other half of sauce. Top casserole with corn flake crumbs. Cook at 350° for 30 minutes.

P.S. For a change, this casserole is good topped with onion rings.

P.P.S. If necessary, you can use canned shrimp.

Avocado Soufflé

¼ cup butter
¼ cup flour
1 cup milk
¾ teaspoon salt
⅛ teaspoon white pepper
⅛ teaspoon nutmeg
¼ teaspoon hot pepper sauce
4 egg yolks
1½ cups very ripe avocados
6 egg whites
Pinch cream of tartar

Butter and flour 6 cup soufflé dish. In a saucepan, melt butter and stir in flour. Cook, stirring constantly for about 3 minutes until bubbly. Add milk, stirring constantly until mixture thickens. Add salt, pepper, nutmeg and hot pepper sauce. Cool. Add egg yolks one at a time beating after each addition. Mash avocados and add to mixture.

In mixer bowl, beat egg whites with cream of tartar until stiff. Fold beaten egg whites into avocado mixture. Pour into prepared soufflé dish and bake in bottom third of 350° preheated oven until top is brown, about 35 minutes. Serve immediately with Lemon Sauce.

Lemon Sauce:

8 oz. cream cheese, softened
2 tablespoons dry white wine
4 tablespoons lemon juice
4 tablespoons chopped
    parsley
3 tablespoons chopped chives
½ teaspoon salt
¼ teaspoon white pepper

Beat cream cheese, wine and lemon juice until smooth. Add remaining ingredients. Serve at room temperature.

Note: Mix leftover Lemon Sauce half and half with Lemon Mayonnaise, adjust seasoning and pour over cut raw vegetables (cauliflower, cucumber, celery, etc.), toss and serve on lettuce leaf. Makes an interesting salad.

To ripen avocados, or tomatoes, put in a brown bag in a dark place —

Bean Bundles

2 cans vertical packed green
   beans
½ lb. bacon

Drain beans. Divide into bundles of 8 or 10 beans. Cut slice of bacon in half, wrap around beans and secure with a toothpick. Put on hot broiler pan and broil until bacon is cooked.

Sauce:

6 tablespoons butter
½ teaspoon salt
1 tablespoon chopped parsley
4 tablespoons tarragon
   vinegar
1 teaspoon pepper
1 teaspoon onion juice
½ teaspoon garlic salt

Combine ingredients and simmer until hot. Serve over bean bundles.

P.S. These are attractive for a dinner party. Arrange the bean bundles on a pretty platter. Decorate your platter with parsley and wedges of tomato or with parsley and pimiento.

Broccoli Casserole

½ cup butter
3 medium onions, sliced
¾ cup chopped celery
¾ cup chicken stock
1 (10 oz.) package frozen
   broccoli
⅓ cup lemon juice
1 teaspoon salt
1 tablespoon cornstarch
2 tablespoons water
2 eggs, beaten
Parmesan cheese

Put butter in large skillet, add onions and celery. Stir until vegetables begin to brown. Add the chicken stock, lemon juice, broccoli and salt. Simmer covered for about 8 minutes. Remove vegetables to oven proof bowl and keep warm. To liquid in skillet add cornstarch mixed with water and cook about 1 minute. Stir some of hot liquid into beaten eggs, then return to skillet and cook over low heat until thickened. Pour over vegetables and sprinkle with Parmesan cheese.

P.S. A good broccoli dish.

Beans and Sauce

16 oz. green beans
1 large sliced onion
Ham or bacon bits

Cook together until tender. Remove cooked onion and bacon or ham, drain beans well. Place in serving bowl and pour the following sauce over top:

Sauce:

Blend all ingredients thoroughly.

1 cup Lemon Mayonnaise
2 chopped boiled eggs
1 heaping tablespoon
  horseradish
1 teaspoon Worcestershire
  sauce
Salt and pepper to taste
Garlic salt and onion salt to
  taste
Juice of one lemon
1 teaspoon parsley flakes

P.S. I like the flavor of Blue Lake green beans with this recipe.

P.P.S. It's hard to find a vegetable dish that is different, but this is.

Green Bean Casserole

16 oz. French cut green beans
1 cup bean sprouts
1 cup water chestnuts
1 (4 oz.) can chopped pimiento
1 sliced onion
1 cup fresh mushrooms
½ cup slivered almonds
2½ cups heavy cheese sauce

In bottom of a casserole, place a layer of green beans, then half of the bean sprouts, water chestnuts, and mushrooms. Then add all the onion and pimiento and half of the cheese sauce. Season with salt and pepper to taste and repeat the process with the rest of the ingredients. Cover the top with almonds and bake in moderate oven for about an hour. Serves 8.

Note: This is different and has a distinctive flavor.

Broccoli Mold

20 oz. chopped broccoli
3 tablespoons butter
3 tablespoons flour
¼ cup chicken broth
1 cup sour cream
⅓ cup minced green onions
3 eggs
¾ cup grated Swiss cheese
½ cup slivered almonds,
   toasted
½ teaspoon pepper
1 teaspoon salt
½ teaspoon nutmeg (optional)

Cook broccoli in 1 cup salted water until tender. Drain thoroughly and chop fine. (Do not use food processor or blender).

Heat butter in skillet and blend in flour. Add chicken broth and sour cream gradually. Stir in onions and cook over low heat, stirring until thick and blended. Beat eggs lightly and stir in some of the hot sauce. Slowly add to mixture in skillet and cook 1 minute. Blend in cheese, add broccoli, almonds and seasonings. Pour into 1 qt. buttered ring mold. Place mold in pan containing about 1½″ hot water. Bake at 350° for about 50 minutes until set. Unmold and sprinkle toasted almonds and parsley over the top.

P.S. You can use individual molds if you prefer. Bake them about 30 minutes. Sprinkle chopped parsley on top before serving. They look pretty when you are having guests for dinner, and they are good!

Brussels Sprouts and Artichokes

2 (10 oz.) packages frozen
   Brussels sprouts
1 (14 oz.) can artichoke hearts,
   drained
⅔ cup Lemon Mayonnaise
½ cup Parmesan cheese
¼ cup melted margarine
3½ tablespoons lemon juice
1 teaspoon celery salt
Sliced almonds (optional)

Cook Brussels sprouts according to package directions. Drain. Slice artichokes and put in bottom of casserole. Cover with Brussels sprouts. Mix remaining ingredients and spoon over vegetables. Cook until bubbly.

P.S. Sprinkle top with sliced almonds if desired.

Broccoli and Onions Deluxe

2 (10 oz.) packages frozen cut
   broccoli
2 cups frozen whole small
   onions
2 tablespoons butter
2 tablespoons flour
½ teaspoon salt
Dash pepper
¾ cup milk
3 oz. cream cheese, cut up
½ cup dry white wine
Toasted sliced almonds

Cook broccoli and onions until tender, about 10 minutes. Melt butter. Blend in flour, salt and pepper. Add milk all at once, cook and stir until bubbly. Blend in cream cheese until smooth. Remove from heat, stir in wine. Fold in vegetables. Turn into casserole. Bake uncovered at 350° for about 30 minutes. Sprinkle almonds over top. Makes 8 servings.

Brussels Sprouts Casserole

1 (10 oz.) package frozen
   Brussels sprouts
½ cup water chestnuts, sliced
¼ cup crisp crumbled bacon
4 tablespoons butter, melted
   and slightly browned
3 tablespoons lemon juice
Parmesan cheese, grated

Cook Brussels sprouts until almost tender. Arrange in shallow casserole, alternating a row of Brussels sprouts and row of water chestnuts. Sprinkle with bacon and pour over the vegetables browned butter to which lemon juice has been added. Sprinkle lightly with Parmesan cheese and cook in 325° oven until well heated.

P.S. This makes an uninteresting vegetable a little more interesting.

add pinch of baking soda to green vegetables and they will retain their color.

Carrots in Orange Juice

6 medium sized fresh carrots
½ to ¾ cup orange juice
1 tablespoon brown sugar
2 tablespoons butter
1 tablespoon grated orange rind

Peel and cut fresh carrots in half, then in strips, lengthwise. Put in saucepan and cover with orange juice. Add butter, brown sugar and orange rind. Cover pan and steam until carrots are tender.

P.S. This is a colorful, attractive vegetable to serve at a dinner party. It goes very nicely with lamb.

Chinese Casserole

1 cup milk
2 tablespoons cornstarch
½ cup margarine
1 teaspoon salt
1 small onion, chopped
⅓ cup chopped celery
2 tablespoons butter
¼ lb. chopped mushrooms
3 tablespoons flour
Salt and pepper to taste
1 cup chicken broth
½ cup light cream
1 (14 oz.) can chop suey vegetables
16 oz. French cut green beans
6 hard boiled eggs, sliced
1 cup slivered almonds
Bread crumbs
Grated cheese

Drain vegetables. Cook together milk, corn starch, margarine, salt, onion and celery until thick. In saucepan melt butter, sauté mushrooms, blend in flour, salt and pepper. Add chicken broth and light cream all at once. Cook over medium heat, stirring constantly until mixture thickens. Combine sauces with other ingredients and mix. Pour into a baking dish and sprinkle with bread crumbs and grated cheese. Bake at 350° for 30 minutes.

When steaming vegetables, put chicken, or beef bouillon cube in water —

Shoe Peg Corn Casserole

¼ cup chopped celery
3 tablespoons butter
3 tablespoons flour
¼ teaspoon salt
Pepper
1¼ cups chicken broth
2 tablespoons light cream
1 (16 oz.) can shoe peg corn
½ cup chopped onion
¼ cup chopped green pepper
½ cup chopped celery
1 cup French style green beans
8 oz. sour cream
Salt and pepper to taste

Topping:

3 cups cracker crumbs
1 stick of margarine, melted

Sauté celery in butter until tender and remove from pan. Blend in flour, salt and pepper. Add chicken broth and cream all at once. Cook over medium heat, stirring constantly until mixture thickens. Add celery and mix with other ingredients. Pour into long flat casserole. Cover with topping. Bake at 350° for 45 minutes. Serves 4 - 6.

Stuffed Eggplant

1 medium sized eggplant
1 cup chopped onion
1 cup chopped fresh
  mushrooms
1¼ teaspoons basil (or
  oregano)
1 teaspoon salt
2 tablespoons butter
1 cup cooked ground beef
½ cup dry bread crumbs

Wash eggplant and wrap in foil. Bake in 350° oven until almost done (about 50 minutes). Cut eggplant in half. Remove pulp to within ½ inch of outer skin. Reserve pulp. Cook onions, mushrooms and seasonings in butter. Add eggplant pulp, beef and bread crumbs. Spoon into shells and put in casserole. Bake until well heated. Serves 2.

P.S. With a pasta dish, this makes a nice meal.

Eggplant and Oysters

1 medium sized eggplant
Pinch oregano
4 tablespoons chopped onions
¼ cup butter
½ cup dry bread crumbs
1 pint oysters
½ cup light cream
Salt and pepper
Hot pepper sauce

Peel, cube and boil eggplant in salted water with oregano. Drain. Sauté onion in butter. Add onions and bread crumbs to eggplant. Heat oysters in small saucepan until edges curl. Drain and add to eggplant mixture, stirring with a fork. Add cream. Season with salt, pepper and hot pepper sauce to taste. Pour into a 2 qt. casserole and cover with additional bread crumbs. Bake at 350° for 15 minutes. Serves 8.

P.S. Do not overcook the eggplant as it will cook more in the casserole. I like to make my own bread crumbs from buttered toast—they taste much better than commercial crumbs.

Eggplant and Shrimp Casserole

1 large eggplant
½ lb. raw shrimp, peeled
1 cup chopped green pepper
1 grated onion
½ cup cracker crumbs
1 tablespoon butter
½ teaspoon Worcestershire
  sauce
⅛ teaspoon red pepper
⅛ teaspoon black pepper
¼ teaspoon salt
½ cup grated sharp cheese
½ cup cream of mushroom
  soup
Parmesan cheese

Peel eggplant and cut into cubes. Boil until soft. Drain. Put eggplant and other ingredients in buttered casserole. Mix well and bake at 325° for 45 minutes. Sprinkle with Parmesan cheese before serving. Serves 6-8.

Macaroni Ring Mold

1½ cups cooked macaroni
1 cup milk
1 egg, beaten
1 cup sharp cheese, grated
1 cup bread crumbs
3 tablespoons chopped
   pimiento
1 teaspoon minced onion
1 teaspoon chopped parsley
1 teaspoon salt
½ teaspoon black pepper

Mix together and bake in buttered ring mold until thoroughly set. Turn onto platter and fill center with peas and mushrooms or any desired vegetable or meat combination. Garnish with parsley. Serves 8.

Note: This is easy, cheap and looks pretty. Doesn't taste too bad either!

Mushrooms in Sherried Cream Sauce

1 lb. fresh mushrooms
4 tablespoons butter
2 tablespoons flour
¾ teaspoon salt
⅛ teaspoon pepper
1 cup half and half cream
1½ tablespoons dry sherry
Toast points

Rinse, pat dry, and cut mushrooms in halves, if large. In large skillet, melt butter, add mushrooms, and sauté until golden (about 5 minutes). Stir in flour, salt and black pepper. Gradually add cream and sherry. Simmer until thick, stirring often. Serve on toast points.

P.S. This is good with a slice of roast or ham, a green vegetable and a salad.

Wild Rice Casserole

1 package long grain and wild
   rice
1 bell pepper, chopped
1 onion, chopped
½ cup margarine
½ cup almonds
1 can (10 oz.) undiluted cream
   of mushroom soup
4 oz. chopped pimientos

Cook rice according to package directions. Sauté pepper and onion in margarine. Add almonds, mushroom soup and pimientos. Bake covered at 325° about 1 hour.

P.S. A good rice casserole!

Gourmet Noodles

½ cup butter
½ lb. sliced mushrooms
¼ cup chopped onion
¼ cup sliced almonds
1 clove garlic, minced
1 tablespoon lemon juice
1 can beef broth
4 oz. medium noodles
Chopped parsley

Melt butter. Add mushrooms, onions, almonds and garlic. Cook about 10 minutes over low heat. Add remaining ingredients and cook until noodles are tender. Sprinkle with chopped parsley.

P.S. Since I'm not a potato lover, any pasta dish interests me. Try this with roast.

Onion Rings or Fried Corn on the Cob

1½ cups plus 2 tablespoons
  beer
1 tablespoon baking powder
1 tablespoon seasoned salt
1 egg
1½ cups flour
Oil for deep frying
2 large Spanish onions, cut
  into ¼" to ½" slices

Combine beer, baking powder, salt and egg in large bowl, and stir well. Gradually add mixture to flour, stirring well to make batter. Heat oil to about 375°. Separate onion rings. Dip in batter and fry in batches until golden brown.

P.S. Jeanne, I know you "don't fry," but try this recipe once and you may start!

P.P.S. I also use this batter to fry corn on the cob. I buy the little frozen corn on the cob, cook according to directions for about 4½ minutes then drop them in ice water for a second. I pat them dry, dip them in batter and fry them until golden brown. Try them, I think you will love them.

Onions in Cream

1½ cups small white onions
½ cup white wine,
   approximately
4 tablespoons butter
Salt and pepper
Bay leaf
Pinch of thyme
Pinch of sweet basil
½ cup light cream
Toasted bread crumbs

Put peeled onions in saucepan. Cover with white wine and add butter and seasonings. Steam until tender. Pour into casserole. Cover with cream and top with toasted bread crumbs. Heat until slightly brown. Serves 6-8.

P.S. Do not use canned onions. We like this with a lamb or beef roast.

Pea Soufflé Ring

1 (17 oz.) can peas
1 onion, quartered
3 egg yolks
2½ tablespoons flour
Milk
1 cup cream
Dash of Worcestershire sauce
Salt and pepper to taste
3 egg whites, stiffly beaten

Cook peas with the onion for about ½ hour. Remove onion and purée peas. Beat egg yolks and add the flour which has been made into a paste with milk. Beat. Add cream, Worcestershire, salt and pepper to pea mixture and fold in stiffly beaten egg whites. Pour into greased ring mold. Put ring mold in 1½ to 2 inches of hot water in pan, and start cooking in oven which has been heated to 400°. Cook 10 minutes and lower to 350° and continue cooking for 35 minutes, adding water to pan if necessary. Serves 6-8.

Note: If you are lucky, this will come out on the platter and you can fill with any desired mixture, such as onions in cream, carrots, mushrooms, etc. It is an attractive dish to serve when you have dinner guests.

Baked Stuffed Potatoes

8 medium Idaho potatoes
8 tablespoons butter
Salt
Pepper
8 tablespoons half and half,
  approximately

Put potatoes in 400° oven and bake until soft to touch. (Do not cook in aluminum foil.) When done, cut a thin slice off long side of each potato. With a spoon, carefully remove potato (leaving potato hull intact). Save potato hulls. Put potato in mixing bowl and beat on low speed, adding butter and salt and pepper to taste. Warm cream and slowly add until potatoes are the consistency of *soft* mashed potatoes. Beat until light. With spoon, carefully refill potato hulls. At this stage, you can cool potatoes and freeze, put in the ice box and keep for a day or two, or better, reheat until lightly browned and eat now.

P.S. This is a simple recipe, but I couldn't write a recipe book for the family without it.

P.P.S. You can pep these up by sprinkling cheese on the top when you reheat them.

Dirty Rice

¾ cup wild rice
2 cups beef broth
½ cup chopped onions
¼ cup chopped green peppers
½ cup chopped mushrooms
3 tablespoons butter, softened
½ cup heavy cream
Salt and pepper to taste

Wash rice and cook in beef broth (or bouillon) until most of liquid has been absorbed. Sauté onions, peppers and mushrooms in butter. Add cream and seasonings. Combine with cooked rice and pour into casserole. Bake at 350° for 20 minutes.

P.S. This is good with quail!

Brandied Sweet Potatoes

4 large sweet potatoes or yams
2 eggs
¼ cup cream, approximately
2 teaspoons cinnamon
¼ teaspoon nutmeg
Sugar
4 tablespoons brandy or rum
Pecan halves and cherries

Boil potatoes until soft. Peel, put in mixing bowl and beat with electric mixer. Add eggs, cream, spices and sugar to taste. Beat until light (should be the consistency of thick batter). Stir in liquor. Taste. Add more liquor if necessary! Pour into casserole and cover with topping. Bake in moderate oven (350°) until topping has browned slightly.

Topping:

½ cup butter
1 cup brown sugar
½ cup flour
1 cup chopped pecans
1 teaspoon vanilla

Blend together and sprinkle over casserole.

P.S. This casserole is best when made with the large, more orange colored potatoes rather than with the smaller, pale yellow ones. The names are confusing though. In the South, the ones I am talking about are just called sweet potatoes; in some other parts of the country, they are called yams. So, don't rely on the name, look at the vegetable before you buy.

P.P.S. This casserole is almost our "trademark" as we are expected to serve it on all major holidays. This turns the lowly "yam" into a gourmet dish.

Boil Corn with a little sugar in the water — Salt will toughen the Corn

Rice Ring

3 egg yolks, beaten
¾ cup finely minced parsley
2 tablespoons Parmesan
  cheese
1 small onion, minced
1 teaspoon salt
1 teaspoon pepper
1 teaspoon paprika
2 tablespoons Worcestershire
  sauce
3 cups cooked rice
3 egg whites

Add egg yolks, parsley, cheese, onion and seasonings to rice. Beat egg whites until stiff and fold into rice mixture. Pour into a buttered ring mold. Put mold in a pan in about 1″ of water and bake in a moderate oven (325°) until set. Unmold and fill with peas, carrots, or any vegetable you like.

P.S. This has always been very difficult for me to unmold so I tried putting plastic wrap in the buttered mold. Butter that too and let it extend over the sides of mold. When you are ready to unmold the ring, it will slip out. How about that?

Squash Casserole Henrietta Grayer

5 medium sized yellow squash
1 small onion, chopped
Salt and pepper to taste
3 eggs
1 tablespoon cornstarch
¼ cup melted butter
1 cup grated cheese

Cut squash in 1″ pieces and boil with onion, salt and pepper. Drain. Beat eggs and cornstarch, add butter, cheese, squash and onions. Put into large mixing bowl and beat until light. Season to taste. Pour into 2 qt. casserole and bake at 350° for 30 minutes.

P.S. This is Henrietta's original recipe for yellow squash and it is very good.

Squash and Green Pepper Casserole

1 cup milk, scalded
1 cup packaged, seasoned
  bread crumbs
3 tablespoons butter
2 cups cooked squash
  (mashed)
½ teaspoon salt
½ teaspoon pepper
1 green pepper, chopped
2 eggs, well beaten

Combine milk, butter, bread crumbs. Add remaining ingredients. Mix and pour into buttered casserole. Bake at 350° for about 25 minutes, or until set.

Zucchini Casserole

8 oz. HOT sausage
4 medium sized zucchini
½ cup grated Parmesan
  cheese
½ cup bread crumbs
1 tablespoon chopped parsley
½ teaspoon garlic salt
⅛ teaspoon pepper
3 egg yolks
2 tablespoons water
3 egg whites
Paprika
Chopped parsley

Brown sausage, remove from fat and drain well. Remove ends from zucchini and cook in boiling salted water about 8 minutes. Drain. Cut 4 thin slices zucchini, set aside. Finely chop remaining zucchini. In large bowl mix zucchini, cheese and all but 2 tablespoons of the bread crumbs. Add sausage, parsley and seasonings. Mix together. Beat egg yolks with water and stir into mixture. Wash beaters and beat egg whites to stiff peaks and fold in. Turn into ungreased 1½ qt. casserole. Sprinkle with reserved bread crumbs and paprika. Garnish with reserved zucchini slices. Bake uncovered in 325° oven for 50 minutes or until set. Sprinkle with parsley before serving. Serves 6-8.

P.S. This could be used as a main course.

Zucchini Casserole #2

1 cup milk
3 eggs, beaten
½ cup butter, melted
2 cups grated cheese
3 cups sliced raw zucchini
4 oz. diced pimiento
1½ cups cracker crumbs
Salt and pepper to taste

Mix milk, eggs, butter and cheese. Add zucchini, pimiento, cracker crumbs and seasonings. Mix well. Pour into greased 2 qt. casserole. Bake, uncovered, in slow oven (300°) for 30-40 minutes, until golden brown. Serves 8.

Zucchini Mold

2 tablespoons butter
2 medium tomatoes, peeled
  and chopped fine
½ teaspoon basil
2 cups zucchini, sliced thin
3 egg yolks
1 egg
1 cup heavy cream
¼ teaspoon hot pepper sauce
¼ teaspoon nutmeg

Butter 6 custard cups. Melt butter in skillet and add tomatoes and basil. Cook until soft, stirring constantly. Put zucchini in boiling water, blanch for 2 minutes, remove to ice water for a few seconds. Pat dry and lightly salt. Divide zucchini and tomatoes evenly into custard cups. Combine yolks and egg in bowl, beat slightly and add cream, salt, pepper, hot pepper sauce and nutmeg. Blend well. Pour cream mixture over vegetables. Place custard cups in pan of hot water that comes about half way up the sides of cups. Bake in 375° oven until custard is set (about 35 minutes). Remove from oven and let sit at room temperature for a few minutes. Unmold and sprinkle with chopped parsley and a dash of nutmeg. Serves 6.

P.S. Very attractive to serve.

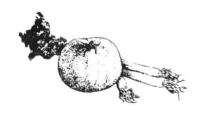

Desserts
and Pastries

Almond Torte

4 stale lady fingers
½ lb. almonds
7 egg yolks
1 cup sugar
2 teaspoons lemon juice
Grated rind of ½ lemon
7 egg whites, well beaten
½ pint heavy cream, whipped
Strawberries (optional)

Toast and pulverize lady fingers. Grind almonds in blender or food processor. Cream yolks of eggs with sugar until very light. Add lady fingers, almonds, lemon juice and rind, and lastly fold in well beaten whites. Bake in two 9″ round pans, which have been greased and floured, in 325° oven for 15-20 minutes until medium brown. Layers are apt to fall a bit when removed from the oven, but that is all right. Cool thoroughly. To serve, ice with sweetened whipped cream between layers and on top. Serves 12 to 14.

P.S. Sliced strawberries covering the top add greatly to this dessert.

Apricot Ice Cream, Julia

1 (17 oz.) can apricots
2½ cups sugar
10 marshmallows
Juice of 4 lemons
1 qt. milk
½ teaspoon almond flavoring
1 pint cream, whipped
2 egg whites, beaten

Drain apricots and put through sieve. Heat sugar, apricots and marshmallows on medium heat, and stir until marshmallows are melted. Cool in bowl in ice box. When thoroughly chilled, add lemon juice, milk and flavoring. Fold in whipped cream and beaten egg whites. Freeze.

P.S. I'm very fond of apricots and I think this ice cream is delicious.

Angel Pie

Meringue:

4 egg whites
¼ teaspoon cream of tartar
1 cup sugar

Beat egg whites until frothy. Add cream of tartar and beat until stiff. Very gradually add sugar and continue beating until very, very stiff. Line cookie sheet with heavy brown paper and spread meringue evenly in an oblong about 1″ thick. Preheat oven to 250°, bake at that heat for 10 minutes. Increase heat to 300° and bake for 40 minutes longer. Peel meringue from paper before it cools.

Filling:

4 egg yolks
2 tablespoons grated lemon rind
½ cup sugar
5 tablespoons lemon juice
½ pint whipping cream

Mix egg yolks, grated lemon rind and sugar. Beat until frothy, then gradually add lemon juice. Put in top of double boiler and cook very slowly until mixture thickens. Cool and fold in stiffly beaten cream. Cut the meringue into 2 layers, spread mixture over bottom layer, add top layer, and cover with remaining mixture. Let stand in refrigerator at least 24 hours.

P.S. This was known as Devil's Pie until I learned to make it!

Bourbon Dessert

40 marshmallows (large)
1 cup milk
1 pint cream, whipped
½ cup Bourbon

Melt marshmallows in milk. Cool. Fold in whipped cream and—last but not least—the Bourbon. Pour into sherbet cups and put in refrigerator until firm. Sprinkle a little nutmeg and, if you like, ground nuts over the top.

P.S. Easy and the flavor is not bad!

Chocolate Mousse

½ lb. semi-sweet chocolate
6 large eggs, separated
3 tablespoons water
¼ cup orange Cognac
2 cups heavy cream
6 tablespoons sugar
Whipped cream
Grated chocolate

Cut chocolate in pieces and melt over boiling water. Put egg yolks in heavy saucepan and add water. Place pan over very low heat while beating constantly with a wire whisk. When yolks begin to thicken, add liqueur, beating constantly. Cook until about the consistency of Hollandaise sauce. Remove from heat. Fold melted chocolate into sauce. Scrape sauce into mixing bowl. Beat cream until stiff, adding 2 tablespoons sugar. Fold into chocolate mixture. Beat egg whites until stiff adding remaining sugar. When stiff, fold into mousse. Spoon into crystal bowl and chill. Garnish with whipped cream and grated chocolate.

P.S. I often fill my parfait glasses with this and leave them in the ice box until the mousse is all gone. Doesn't take long.

Chocolate Pudding Libby

1 egg
½ cup sugar
½ cup milk
1 cup flour
3 tablespoons cocoa
1½ teaspoons baking powder
¼ teaspoon salt
1 tablespoon melted butter
1 teaspoon vanilla

Beat egg and add sugar and milk. Then add sifted dry ingredients and melted butter. Add vanilla and pour into buttered mold and bake in moderate oven. Serve with chocolate sauce made from equal portions of fudge sauce (see recipe) and whipped cream.

Chocolate Mousse Mandarin

1 cup semi-sweet chocolate
　chips
1 cup whipping cream
¼ cup sugar
2 egg yolks
1 teaspoon gelatine
1 tablespoon water
2 tablespoons orange liqueur
1 tablespoon brandy
2 teaspoons grated orange
　rind
2 egg whites
2 tablespoons sugar

Melt chocolate and allow to cool. Put whipping cream, melted chocolate, ¼ cup sugar and egg yolks in blender, cover and blend until smooth and slightly thickened. Soak gelatine in water. Stir over heat until melted. Add gelatine to orange liqueur and brandy. Add gelatine, liqueur, brandy and orange rind to mixture in blender. Beat egg whites until stiff, add 2 tablespoons sugar and fold beaten whites into chocolate mixture. Pour into pots de crème or sherbet cups. Chill several hours. Serve with whipped cream and sliced almonds. Makes 6-8 servings.

P.S. Rich but good.

Stone Cold Coffee

3 oz. coffee liqueur
3 oz. orange liqueur
1 cup heavy cream, whipped
2 cups coffee ice cream,
　softened
Whipped cream for garnish
2 tablespoons toasted almonds

Combine ingredients by folding into ice cream with wire whisk. Pour into parfait glasses and freeze. Serve with a dollop of whipped cream and sprinkle with toasted almond slices. Makes 6 servings.

P.S. Stir several times while freezing or the liquid will sink to the bottom of the glass.

P.P.S. They call this Stone Cold Coffee because if you have seconds you will be stoned cold!

Cold Chocolate Soufflé

2 cups milk
2 envelopes unflavored
   gelatine
¼ teaspoon salt
12 oz. semi-sweet chocolate
   chips
1 cup sugar
4 egg yolks
4 egg whites
1 pint whipping cream
1 teaspoon vanilla
14 lady fingers

Put milk in medium-sized pan. Sprinkle gelatine over milk, add salt, chocolate and ½ cup sugar. Over low heat, stirring constantly, add egg yolks that have been beaten until light. Continue to cook slowly until gelatine and chocolate have melted. Remove from stove and beat with rotary beater. Cool until thick enough to mound when stirred. This is important as it must be cool and of the right consistency for the next step. Beat egg whites until stiff, slowly add remaining sugar, and beat until very stiff. With wire whisk, fold chocolate mixture into egg whites a spoonful at a time. Add heavy cream that has been whipped. Add vanilla. Pour into 9″ springform pan that has been lined with lady fingers.

P.S. Serve on a footed cake stand. Pipe whipped cream around the bottom of the dessert and around the top edge. Decorate with chocolate leaves (see recipe for Chocolate Mousse Pie).

P.P.S. This sounds hard, but if you will follow the directions, it really is not complicated. This is a special family favorite.

Frozen Angel Pie

4 egg whites
½ teaspoon cream of tartar
Pinch of salt
1½ cups sugar
4 egg yolks
Grated rind of 2 lemons
3 tablespoons lemon juice
1 cup whipping cream

Beat egg whites until frothy, add cream of tartar and salt and beat until stiff. Slowly add 1 cup of sugar, a tablespoon at a time. This mixture should be glossy and stand in stiff peaks. With back of spoon spread meringue in well buttered pie pan, pushing high on the sides to form a shell. Bake at 300° for 40 minutes.

Beat egg yolks and the remaining ½ cup of sugar in top of double boiler until light. Stir in lemon rind and juice and cook over hot water until thick, stirring constantly. Chill. With wire whisk add the cream that has been whipped. Pour into meringue shell that has been thoroughly cooled. Freeze.

P.S. I have better luck with my meringue if after 40 minutes, I turn the oven off, crack the door slightly and leave the meringue in the oven for an hour or so.

Fudge Sauce

2 oz. German sweet chocolate
4 oz. unsweetened chocolate
3 tablespoons butter
1 cup sugar
¼ cup corn syrup
⅓ cup cream
Few grains salt
1 teaspoon vanilla
2 tablespoons sherry

Melt chocolate and butter in top of double boiler. Add remaining ingredients and heat, stirring until blended. Serve warm over ice cream or cake.

Chocolate Torte

Meringue:

2 egg whites
½ teaspoon salt
½ teaspoon vinegar
½ cup sugar

Filling:

6 oz. semi-sweet chocolate
2 egg yolks
¼ cup water
1 cup whipping cream
¼ cup sugar
Chopped nuts
Additional whipped cream for
decorating

Cover bottom of cookie sheet with brown paper and draw in the center an 8 inch circle. Combine egg whites, salt and vinegar in bowl and beat together until soft peaks form. Continue beating and add sugar very gradually. Beat until very stiff. Spread meringue with spatula on circle until it is about ½" thick. Build up sides to form a pie shell. Bake at 250° for an hour. Cool thoroughly.

Melt the chocolate in top of double boiler over hot but not boiling water. Cool slightly and spread 2 tablespoons of chocolate over cooled pie shell. Beat egg yolks with water and combine with remaining chocolate. Cook until thick, remove from heat. While this is cooling, beat until stiff the whipping cream and sugar. Spread half of whipped cream over pie shell, combine remainder with chocolate mixture and fill pie shell. Sprinkle with chopped nuts and more whipped cream. Chill several hours and cut into pie shaped pieces.

Note: This is an elegant dessert.

Melt chocolate in slow oven on shaped aluminum foil - Scrape off with rubber spatula —

Chocolate Soufflé

⅓ cup flour
¾ cup sugar
1½ cups milk
3 oz. unsweetened chocolate, grated
6 egg yolks
2 teaspoons vanilla
6 egg whites
¼ teaspoon salt
Sweetened whipped cream

Grease 2 quart soufflé dish (or round glass casserole dish) with butter and sprinkle with sugar. In medium saucepan, measure flour and ¼ cup sugar. With wire whisk slowly stir in milk until smooth. Cook over medium heat, stirring constantly until mixture thickens and comes to a boil. Continue to cook for 1 minute. Remove from heat, stir in chocolate until melted. Rapidly beat in egg yolks (all at once) until well mixed. Add vanilla. Cool, stirring occasionally until lukewarm. Set aside.

In large bowl of mixer, beat egg whites and salt until soft peaks form. Add ½ cup sugar very gradually. Beat until very stiff. With wire whisk stir in chocolate mixture. Pour into soufflé dish. With back of spoon make 1 inch indentation around edge of dish. Bake at 375° for 35 to 40 minutes. Serve at once with sweetened whipped cream.

P.S. Has to be eaten immediately or it will fall.

Chocolate Mousse Pie

3 cups chocolate wafer crumbs
½ cup butter, melted

Mix and press into bottom and sides of 9" springform pan.

Filling:

1 lb. semi-sweet chocolate
2 whole eggs
4 egg yolks
4 egg whites
6 tablespoons powdered sugar
2 cups heavy cream, whipped

Soften chocolate in top of double boiler. Let cool, add whole eggs. Mix until blended and add egg yolks. Beat egg whites until stiff, add powdered sugar, fold whipped cream and egg whites into chocolate mixture, using a wire whisk. Turn into prepared springform pan and chill overnight. Unmold, cut into slices, and serve with sweetened whipped cream and chocolate leaves.

P.S. To make chocolate leaves, melt 3 oz. semi-sweet chocolate with ½ teaspoon butter. Pick waxy leaves, such as camellias or holly leaves (from your garden). With pastry brush, coat back of leaves with a thick layer of chocolate. Chill until hard and carefully peel the leaf away from the chocolate. This takes a little practice, but its worth it.

P.P.S. This recipe is about right for my family of "chocoholics".

Eggs separate easier when cool —

Coffee Cloud Pie

Meringue:

3 egg whites
¾ teaspoon cream of tartar
¾ cup sugar
½ cup ground almonds
½ teaspoon vanilla

Filling:

3 teaspoons instant coffee
½ cup milk
20 large marshmallows
2 egg yolks
1 cup heavy cream
¼ teaspoon almond flavoring
Pinch of salt

Beat egg whites with cream of tartar until stiff. Gradually add sugar, almonds and vanilla. Butter 9″ glass pie pan and spread meringue, building up sides. Bake at 350° for about 40 minutes (or until golden brown). Let cool.

Combine coffee, milk, marshmallows and salt in saucepan. Over low heat stir until marshmallows melt. Remove from heat. Beat egg yolks and stir into hot milk mixture. Return to heat and stirring constantly, cook 1 to 2 minutes. Cool until thick and smooth. Whip cream, add flavoring and fold gently into custard mixture. Pour into crust and freeze.

P.S. Decorate with whipped cream and cherries. Good!

Coffee Ice Cream Dessert

12 to 16 almond macaroons
½ gallon coffee ice cream
Bourbon
Whipped cream

Line a large bowl with almond macaroons, soak in bourbon. Fill bowl with coffee ice cream and put in freezer. A few minutes before serving, take out of freezer and top with whipped cream. Serve from the table.

P.S. This is nice to have on hand for unexpected company.

Ice Cream Bombe

½ gallon coffee ice cream
6 chocolate toffee candy bars, crushed
1 cup flaked coconut, toasted
½ cup heavy cream, whipped

Lightly oil large ice cream mold. Put ice cream about ½″ thick in mold on sides and bottom. Sprinkle crushed candy bars over ice cream (sides and bottom of mold), reserving one fourth for top. Sprinkle with half of toasted coconut. Put in freezer to harden. When frozen, pour following mousse into ice cream mold and return to freezer for mousse to set up. Remove from freezer and sprinkle remaining crushed candy and coconut over mousse. Cover with a layer of ice cream. Return to freezer. When frozen, unmold and decorate with whipped cream and chocolate curls.

Mousse:

½ lb. semi-sweet chocolate
¼ cup water
½ cup sugar
5 egg yolks, beaten
3 tablespoons hot coffee
5 egg whites

Melt the chocolate, add water and ¼ cup sugar in top of double boiler. When melted, stir well and remove from heat. Pour 1 or 2 tablespoons of hot chocolate mixture into well beaten egg yolks. Stir and add hot coffee. Return to heat and stir until mixture thickens. Remove from heat and cool. Beat egg whites, gradually adding remaining sugar, until stiff. Add cooled chocolate mixture to egg whites, folding in carefully with wire whisk. Freeze.

Use a spatula to loosen the edge around the top. You can unmold the bombe the day before you serve it. It will keep well in the freezer for a long time. Serve this dessert at the table by cutting it into slices.

P.S. If you don't have a big ice cream mold, use any large plastic or metal bowl (glass may break). To unmold, turn the mold on a plate and cover it with a hot cloth.

Note: This is a very versatile recipe. There are many variations. Line chilled mold with coffee ice cream. To egg mixture, add 1 cup of praline powder, chill and fold in whipped cream. Pour into the mold. Or, you can use strawberry ice cream to line the mold, and add 1 cup of fresh strawberries to egg mixture, chill and fold in whipped cream. You can make an all chocolate bombe by using chocolate ice cream and adding 4 ounces of melted sweet chocolate to the egg mixture. Another variation is to use vanilla ice cream, adding ⅓ cup of your favorite liqueur to flavor the mousse.

Zabaglione

6 egg yolks
6 tablespoons sugar
⅔ cup Marsala wine

Beat egg yolks with wire whisk and gradually add, while beating, the sugar and wine. Place in saucepan over boiling water, and beat vigorously until custard foams up in pan and begins to thicken. Serve warm in sherbet glasses.

P.S. You can use this recipe as a sauce by adding 2 teaspoons cornstarch to sugar. Good over strawberry shortcake or custards.

147

Baked Custard

3 eggs
½ cup sugar
¼ teaspoon salt
2 cups milk
1 teaspoon vanilla

Combine eggs, sugar and salt. Beat until light. Gradually add milk and vanilla and blend. Pour into 6 well-buttered custard cups. Place cups in shallow pan, and add hot water to ¾" from top of cups. Bake at 350° for 30 minutes or until silver knife inserted comes out clean. Serves 6.

P.S. Sprinkle a dash of nutmeg on top after baked or put a spoonful of jelly or preserves on top.

P.P.S. I double this recipe when my grandaughter, Nancy, comes to see me, for she thinks baked custard and fudge cake are synonymous with grandma's house!

Coffee Tortoni

1 cup small marshmallows
⅓ cup milk
1 teaspoon instant coffee
   powder
¼ cup toasted chopped
   almonds
2 egg whites
½ teaspoon vanilla
2 tablespoons sugar
½ cup whipping cream

In saucepan heat and stir marshmallows, milk and coffee powder until marshmallows are melted. Cool and add chopped almonds. Beat egg whites and vanilla. Add sugar and fold egg whites into coffee mixture. Fold in whipped cream. Spoon into paper cups in muffin pans. Top with cherry and additional almonds. Freeze until firm. 8 cups.

P.S. Nice to have in the freezer when you were not expecting company (or grandchildren)!

Baked Custard Deluxe
(My favorite dessert)

1 cup sugar
½ cup water
4 whole eggs
4 egg yolks
⅛ teaspoon salt
1 cup heavy cream
2½ cups milk
1 teaspoon vanilla

Cook ⅓ cup sugar over low heat until caramelized. Add water and stir until smooth and about the consistency of syrup. Pour caramelized sugar into buttered 1 quart ring mold. Beat together the whole eggs, egg yolks, remaining sugar and salt. Add cream, milk and flavoring. Add a little at a time to caramelized mixture in bottom of mold. Set the mold in a pan of boiling water (about 1½" of water). Bake at 325° until set. (A knife will come out clean). Put into pan of cold water to chill quickly. To unmold, run tip of knife around sides of mold. Place plate over custard, then invert. Shake gently and lift off mold.

Note: This has many possibilities. You can fill the center with whipped cream and fresh strawberries or make a glaze with frozen cherries, raspberries, strawberries or blueberries and cover custard. When I use the fruit glaze, I leave the caramelized sugar off.

Fruit Glaze:

2 tablespoons cornstarch
2 tablespoons orange juice
1 tablespoon lemon juice
1 teaspoon lemon rind
1 teaspoon orange rind

Thicken the juice from thawed frozen fruit with cornstarch. Add orange juice, lemon juice, lemon rind and orange rind. Cook until slightly thickened. If using red fruits, add a drop of red food coloring. Add fruit and pour over custard before serving.

P.S. Can be used as a glaze for cakes, custards or ice cream, also.

Jellied Custard Ring

2 cups milk
4 eggs
½ cup sugar
1 envelope unflavored gelatine
2 teaspoons vanilla

Scald milk. Beat eggs and sugar until light. Gradually add the scalded milk and put in top of double boiler. Cook until mixture coats spoon, remove from fire. Add the gelatine which has been soaked in a little cold water. Add vanilla. Pour into ring mold, cool and let set. Turn mold into chilled platter and fill center with ice cream and strawberries or raspberries and, if you desire, top with whipped cream. Garnish with sprigs of mint. Serve at the table.

Note: This needs no explanation as you have had it so many times at home. If you do not use all of the jellied custard ring the first meal, try it the next day with a sauce made of strawberry preserves.

Macaroon Dessert

4 envelopes gelatine
½ cup cold water
1 cup sherry
8 egg yolks
1 cup sugar
1¼ cups milk
26 almond macaroons, crushed
1 cup chopped nuts
1 cup chopped maraschino cherries
8 egg whites
¾ cup cream, whipped

Soak gelatine in water. Heat sherry and dissolve gelatine in it. Set aside. Beat egg yolks with sugar until thick and add milk that has been scalded. Cook until thick. Add gelatine and crushed macaroons to custard while hot. Cool. When cool, add nuts and cherries to custard and blend in stiffly beaten egg whites and whipped cream. Turn into mold. Serve with spoonful of whipped cream.

P.S. Delicious! I usually make this in individual gelatine molds.

Grasshopper Torte

1½ cups chocolate cookie
  crumbs
Additional thin chocolate
  cookies
½ cup melted butter, approx.
40 marshmallows
1¼ cups half-and-half
½ cup green crème de menthe
⅓ cup white crème de cacao
Few drops green food
  coloring (optional)
2 egg whites
4 tablespoons sugar
1 pint heavy cream

Butter a 9″ springform pan. Mix the cookie crumbs with enough melted butter to make a crust. Press onto the bottom of the pan and as far up the sides as possible. Stand additional whole cookies around the edge to build it up.

Melt the marshmallows with the half-and-half in the top of a double boiler. When cool, add crème de menthe and crème de cacao and the green coloring if you wish. Put aside until it begins to thicken. When cool and thick, beat the egg whites until stiff and slowly add the sugar. Whip the cream until very stiff. With wire whisk, fold the egg whites into the cream and slowly add the marshmallow mixture. Pour into the prepared pan and freeze.

P.S. This makes a beautiful dessert to serve at the table. Put an additional rim of whipped cream on top and some grated chocolate. Keeps well in the freezer.

P.P.S. Be sure to use white crème de cacao!

Never add whipped cream, or beaten egg whites, to a hot mixture —

No Bake Daiquiri Cheese Cake

1¼ cups graham cracker
   crumbs
1¼ cups sugar
6 tablespoons butter, melted
1 envelope gelatine
½ cup rum
2 teaspoons grated lime peel
1 teaspoon grated lemon peel
½ cup lime juice
4 egg yolks, beaten
16 oz. cream cheese, softened
4 egg whites, beaten
1 cup whipping cream

Combine crumbs, ¼ cup sugar and melted butter. Remove 2 tablespoons crumb mixture and set aside. Press remaining crumbs onto bottom and up sides of 9″ springform pan. Chill 45 minutes.

In a saucepan combine gelatine and ½ cup sugar. Stir in the rum, citrus peels, lime juice and egg yolks. Cook over medium heat stirring constantly for 8 to 10 minutes, until slightly thickened. Remove from heat. Beat in cream cheese until smooth. Beat egg whites with remaining ½ cup sugar. Whip cream until stiff. Fold cream and egg whites into gelatine mixture. Turn into prepared pie pan. Sprinkle reserved crumbs around edge. Chill overnight.

Lemon Dessert Squares

Pastry:

1 cup flour
½ cup butter
1 teaspoon salt
¼ cup powdered sugar

Work ingredients together until meal-like consistency. Press into a 9″ square pan and bake 20 minutes at 350°.

Filling:

2 eggs, well beaten
1 cup sugar
1 teaspoon baking powder
3 tablespoons lemon juice
4 tablespoons flour
½ teaspoon grated lemon rind

Mix well and pour over hot crust. Bake at 350° for 25 minutes. Cut into small squares and sprinkle with powdered sugar.

P.S. These are so good! Little lemon pies!

Lemon Bavarian Dessert

13 lady fingers
8 egg yolks
½ cup lemon juice
Rinds of 2 lemons, grated
2 cups sugar
2 envelopes gelatine
½ cup water
8 egg whites

Butter sides of springform pan, line with split lady fingers (it may take more than 13). Beat egg yolks, add lemon juice, rind and 1 cup sugar. Cook in double boiler until it thickens. Add gelatine, soaked in water. Stir until gelatine is dissolved. Cool thoroughly. Beat egg whites stiff and add remaining cup of sugar. Fold in custard. Pour into pan and refrigerate until set. Serve with whipped cream.

P.S. A very light and delicious dessert.

Lemon Custards

⅓ cup flour
1 cup sugar
⅛ teaspoon salt
3 tablespoons butter
3 egg yolks
1 cup milk
3 tablespoons lemon juice
½ teaspoon grated lemon rind
3 egg whites

Sift flour, sugar and salt. Cream into dry ingredients butter and egg yolks. Add milk and beat well. Add lemon juice, lemon rind and stiffly beaten egg whites. Pour into buttered custard cups. Place cups in a pan with about 1 inch water and bake at 350° for about 40 minutes. Turn out of custard cups and serve with whipped cream, or a spoon of ice cream.

Note: The cake mixture sinks to the bottom and will be on top of the custard when you turn these out of the cups. These are light and very good.

Orange Dessert

Crust:

1½ cups graham cracker
crumbs
¼ cup sugar
¼ cup melted butter

Mix the crust and press into bottom of 9″ springform pan.

Filling:

16 oz. cream cheese
3 egg yolks
1 cup orange juice
1 cup sugar
¼ teaspoon salt
2 envelopes unflavored
gelatine
2 teaspoons lemon juice
2 tablespoons grated orange
rind
3 egg whites
1 cup cream, whipped

Soften cream cheese at room temperature and beat until fluffy in large bowl. Set aside. Beat egg yolks in top of double boiler, stir in ½ cup orange juice, sugar and salt. Cook over hot water until slightly thickened; add gelatine that has been soaked in ½ cup orange juice. Add lemon juice and orange rind. When cool, blend in cream cheese. Chill and when mixture begins to set, fold in beaten egg whites and whipped cream. Chill until firm. Garnish with red cherries, or mandarin orange slices, and sprigs of mint.

P.S. This is a pretty dessert—and it tastes pretty good too!

Coconut Crunch Torte

1 cup graham cracker crumbs
½ cup chopped nuts
½ cup shredded coconut
4 egg whites
1 teaspoon vanilla
¼ teaspoon salt
1 cup sugar

Combine crumbs, nuts and coconut. Beat egg whites with vanilla and salt until almost stiff. Gradually add sugar and continue beating until very stiff. Fold in graham cracker mixture. Spread in well buttered 8x11″ pan. Bake at 350° for 30 minutes. Cut in squares and serve with whipped topping.

Meringues

4 egg whites
1 cup sugar
1 teaspoon white vinegar
1 teaspoon vanilla

Beat egg whites until very stiff. Very gradually add sugar and beat until it holds its shape. Add vinegar and vanilla. Line cookie sheet with brown paper. Shape into shells. Use a large soup spoon to make the bottom of each shell and indent it, then put the sides on with a pastry tube. (If you do not have a pastry tube, the rose attachment to your cookie press will do nicely.) Bake at 250° for about an hour. Makes about 11 nice size meringues.

Fill with ice cream, sherbet, lemon or chocolate filling.

Note: When meringues are light brown and dry (should take about an hour), turn oven off, crack oven door, and leave them in the oven for an hour or two. **Do not try to make meringues on a rainy day. They absorb moisture and will be "chewy".**

Strawberry Dessert

1 large angel food cake
2 packages cherry flavored
  gelatine
2 packages frozen
  strawberries
½ gallon vanilla ice cream

Break angel food cake into small bits. Dissolve gelatine in 2 cups hot water. Let cool. Thaw strawberries and mash. Mix gelatine and strawberries. Soften ½ gallon vanilla ice cream. Mix gelatine and strawberries and angel food cake bits into ice cream. Mix well and pour into 11″ tube pan and freeze.

P.S. Slice. Top with whipped cream.

155

Frozen Meringue Velvet

1 cup minced candied fruit
½ cup maraschino syrup or
  orange brandy
1⅔ cups sugar
½ cup water
6 egg whites, beaten stiffly
1¾ cups chopped almonds,
  pecans or pistachio nuts
2 cups heavy cream, whipped

Marinate candied fruit in syrup or brandy until ready to use. In saucepan combine sugar and water. Bring to a boil and cook until it reaches soft ball stage in cold water (236°). Add syrup to beaten egg whites in a thin stream. Continue to beat until mixture forms stiff peaks. Chill. Add nuts and fruit to meringue. Fold in the whipped cream, blending the two mixtures well. Freeze.

P.S. This makes a pretty dessert. Use your wire whisk to fold mixtures. I use orange brandy to marinate the fruit. It doesn't freeze as well with the brandy but it does taste better.

Sherbet Dessert

18 macaroons
½ cup finely chopped nuts
1 pint heavy cream
½ cup sugar
1 teaspoon vanilla
1 pint lime sherbet
1 pint orange sherbet
1 pint grape sherbet

Crush macaroons and mix with chopped nuts. Whip the cream, adding sugar and vanilla. Spread half of crumb mixture on greased 9″ springform pan and mash down for crust. Over this, layer the three sherbets. Allow to freeze partially, spread with whipped cream and add rest of crust on top. Freeze until solid.

Note: Work fast with the sherbet so the layers won't mix too much. So pretty!

Soufflé Glacé Grand Marnier

2 packages lady fingers
3 tablespoons concentrated
   frozen orange juice
1 cup sugar
6 egg yolks
1 tablespoon grated orange
   rind
2½ cups heavy cream
½ cup Grand Marnier

Line side and cover bottom of 9″ springform pan with lady fingers. In saucepan, add orange juice to sugar, stir well and bring to boil over low heat. Stir constantly and boil for a few seconds. Beat egg yolks until very light and thick, slowly add orange juice and orange rind, and allow to cool. Whip cream. Fold whipped cream and ⅓ cup of Grand Marnier into beaten egg yolk mixture. Pour half of mixture over lady fingers in springform pan. Sprinkle remaining lady fingers with remainder of Grand Marnier. Place on top of mixture in pan. Pour in remaining mixture and freeze.

P.S. This is as elegant as its name. Will keep in freezer for a long time.

Fresh Peach Dessert

30 coconut macaroons
2 cups mashed fresh peaches
1 cup sugar, approx.
1 tablespoon lemon juice
1 cup heavy cream, whipped

Crush the macaroons and sprinkle a thick layer in the bottom of a 9″ square pan. Combine the remaining ingredients and pour over the crumb layer. Sprinkle additional crumbs over the top. Freeze. Serve in squares.

P.S. You need to find macaroons that crush well without getting gummy. The amount of sugar you use depends upon how tart your peaches are, so taste before adding all the sugar. I think this is a very good dessert.

Orange Gelatine Dessert

2 tablespoons unflavored
  gelatine
½ cup cold water
½ cup boiling water
⅔ cup strained fresh orange
  juice
1 cup sugar
¼ teaspoon salt
3 tablespoons strained lemon
  juice
¾ cup sherry
Heavy cream

Mix gelatine and cold water. Dissolve in boiling water and add other ingredients. Pour into sherbet cups and let congeal. Serve with heavy (unwhipped) cream.

P.S. A very good finish to a meal.

Pavlova

6 egg whites
12 tablespoons sugar
2 teaspoons vanilla
2 teaspoons white vinegar

Beat egg whites until stiff, gradually adding sugar while beating. Add vanilla and vinegar. Lightly grease a cookie sheet and cover with heavy brown paper. Draw a circle (8″ or 9″) on the brown paper. Mound egg whites on circle, building it up to 2½″ to 3½″, keeping in circle. It will be shaped liked a cake when you finish. Smooth with a spatula. Bake in 200° oven for an hour. Turn off heat and leave in oven another hour or longer. Remove and peel off paper. Place on flat plate. Before serving, frost sides and top with following topping and cover with sliced fruit of your choice.

Note: I like to make my meringue in the afternoon, turn off the heat, and leave it in the oven overnight. It will be dry and crisp the next day when I am ready to serve it.

Topping:

1 pint heavy cream, whipped
1 tablespoon gelatine
3 tablespoons water
Fruit of your choice (kiwis,
  peaches, strawberries, etc.)

Soak gelatine in water and melt over low heat. When gelatine is cool, pour into stiffly whipped cream. Sweeten to taste and flavor with any flavoring you like.

P.S. This dessert is pretty, covered with sliced strawberries. (If you want to get fancy, color your topping pink). When I use strawberries, I flavor the topping with Grand Marnier. You can use sliced peaches, sliced kiwis, dark sweet cherries (drained), orange slices or any fruit you have. Decide what flavoring you like with the fruit you use. Keep in "fridge" several hours before serving so that the topping will set up. The meringue will have a marshmallow-like consistency. Light and delicious!

Fresh Peach Mousse

30 large marshmallows
¼ cup milk
1½ cups puréed fresh peaches
4 tablespoons sugar, approx.
½ pint heavy cream

Melt marshmallows with milk in top of double boiler. Put aside to cool. Purée the peaches and sugar together. Whip the cream until stiff. With wire whisk blend marshmallow mixture, peach purée and whipped cream. Pour into parfait glasses and freeze. Garnish with a small wedge of fresh peach and a sprig of mint when serving.

P.S. I can't tell you how much sugar to add as that will depend on your peaches. Taste after you mix and correct. The marshmallows keep the parfait from becoming icy.

Frozen Oranges

6 large oranges
1 pint orange sherbet
3 tablespoons orange liqueur

Cut slice from top of each orange and with fruit spoon or small knife, remove juice and pulp. Soften the sherbet slightly. Mix sherbet with the liqueur and as much of the pulp and juice as you were able to salvage. Fill the orange shells with the sherbet mixture. Place in a shallow pan and freeze. When frozen, they can be wrapped in aluminum foil and stacked.

P.S. This is easy and a lovely dessert on a hot day. Put a spoonful of whipped cream on before serving and add a sprig of fresh mint. You may have to take a slice off the bottom of the oranges (without making a hole) to make them sit evenly.

Tipsy Pudding

1 (17 oz.) can Bing cherries
½ cup Bourbon
24 almond macaroons
½ gallon vanilla ice cream

Combine the cherries and juice with the Bourbon. Let stand overnight. Crush the macaroons and add to softened ice cream. Stir in the cherry mixture and freeze.

Note: I serve this in parfait glasses with whipped cream between layers of pudding. Because of the alcohol content, this does not freeze very hard. It tastes good for the same reason!

Strawberry Meringue Dessert

Meringues:

4 egg whites
1 cup sugar
Pinch salt
½ teaspoon cream of tartar

Dessert and sauce:

1 quart vanilla ice cream
1 quart fresh strawberries
1 cup red currant jelly
2 tablespoons Cognac

Beat egg whites with sugar until very stiff, adding salt and cream of tartar. Drop by spoonfuls on brown paper and bake at 250° for 1 to 1½ hours. Cool. This makes lots of little meringue balls.

In a large pretty bowl, put ice cream, strawberries and mix into this your meringue balls (it doesn't take all of them). For sauce, melt jelly in top of double boiler and add cognac.

Serve dessert from the table in sherbet glasses and pour over the top 1 or 2 spoonfuls of warm jelly sauce. A truly elegant dessert!

P.S. I also use the jelly and Cognac over baked custard, ice cream, etc.

P.P.S. The extra meringue balls can be stored in an airtight container in the ice box or in the freezer.

When heating egg whites be very sure your bowl is clean and dry.

Marbled Strawberry Mousse

3 pints strawberries, hulled
3 envelopes unflavored
  gelatine
¾ cup sugar
⅛ teaspoon salt
¾ cup water
2 tablespoons lemon juice
1 teaspoon vanilla
4 egg whites
2 cups heavy cream

Tape 3″ wide foil strip outside 1½ quart soufflé dish to make 2″ wide collar above rim. In blender purée berries. Pour 1 cup of the purée into small bowl and the remainder into a large bowl. In saucepan, mix gelatine, sugar and salt. Add water, cook over low heat until gelatine is dissolved, stirring often. Into purée in small bowl, stir 1 tablespoon gelatine mixture. Into purée in large bowl, stir lemon juice, vanilla and remaining gelatine mixture. Refrigerate this mixture, stirring often until it mounds when dropped from a spoon.

    In another large bowl beat egg whites at high speed until stiff. In another small bowl at medium speed beat cream until soft peaks form. Fold whites and whipped cream with wire whisk alternately into strawberry mixture in large bowl. Add reserved cup of purée. Spoon mixture into soufflé dish. With knife cut through to make a swirled design. Refrigerate.

P.S. Good and pretty!

Sherried Strawberries

4 egg yolks
1 envelope gelatine
2 to 4 tablespoons sherry
⅔ cup sugar
1 cup heavy cream
1 pint fresh strawberries,
   sliced

Beat egg yolks and sugar until light. Put in top of double boiler and cook, stirring constantly until sugar is melted and mixture thickens. Remove from heat. Soak gelatine in sherry, add to hot mixture and stir until gelatine has melted. Put aside and cool. Whip cream until stiff and add cooled custard mixture to whipped cream. Carefully add sliced strawberries and pour into crystal bowl or individual sherbet cups. Refrigerate several hours.

P.S. I put my strawberry slices in a bowl with a little additional sherry before I add them to the custard. Serve with Madeleines.

Vanilla Bavarian Cream Pie

1⅛ tablespoons gelatine
8 tablespoons cold water
9 tablespoons sugar
2 eggs, lightly beaten
1½ cups scalded milk
¼ cup vanilla ice cream
1 teaspoon vanilla
2 cups heavy cream, whipped
2¼ tablespoons cornstarch
9″ pie shell, baked

Soften gelatine in cold water. In bowl combine sugar and eggs and mix well. Stir in cornstarch. Add milk and gelatine, stirring. Cook in double boiler until custard thickens and coats the spoon. Remove from heat. Add ice cream while custard is hot. Cool thoroughly. Add vanilla and fold in most of the whipped cream. Pour into shell. Chill. Garnish with remaining whipped cream.

Almond Paste Crust
For Small Swedish Timbals

7 tablespoons softened butter
¾ cup, plus 2 tablespoons
    flour
2½ teaspoons potato starch
    (cornstarch will do)
¼ cup sugar
3 to 4 tablespoons almond
    paste (heaping)
½ teaspoon almond flavoring

Combine all ingredients in bowl, work like pie crust. Pinch off marble size pieces and shape in timbal pans. Press in. Bake at 350°. Fill with cream filling. Top with cherry and sour cream.

Cream Filling:

1 cup heavy cream
3 tablespoons flour or
    cornstarch
6 tablespoons sugar
Pinch salt
1 egg
1 tablespoon vanilla

Scald the cream. Cool. Mix flour with sugar and salt. Beat egg well and add cream. Blend into dry ingredients and cook in double boiler, stirring constantly, until thick and smooth. Cool and add flavoring. Refrigerate until ready to use.

Rich Pastry

2 cups flour
⅛ teaspoon salt
2 egg yolks, beaten
¾ cup butter, softened
2 tablespoons water

Place flour and salt in bowl. Make well in center, put in beaten egg yolks, butter and water. Mix with fingers until it becomes a ball. Chill well before rolling. Cook in 400° oven until brown. Makes one 9″ pie shell.

P.S. You can use this for pie, tarts or pastry for hors d'oeuvres.

Rich Pie Crust

⅓ cup shortening
⅓ cup butter
2 cups sifted all-purpose flour
½ teaspoon salt
1 teaspoon fine granulated
sugar
4 to 6 tablespoons ice water

Blend shortening and butter at room temperature. Sift dry ingredients into bowl and put in refrigerator until well chilled. Blend in shortening with pastry blender or two knives until like small peas. Sprinkle ice water, 2 tablespoons at a time, over flour mixture, tossing with a fork. When dough holds together, divide into 2 equal parts and wrap in foil and chill for at least two hours. This makes one 9″ pie crust with top or 12 tart shells. Grease pie pan or tart shells with shortening and dust with a little flour.

P.S. This is a delicious pie crust. Use it for fruit pies or for tart shells for individual pies. When I make fruit pies, I make a lattice top.

Basic Pie Crust

2 cups flour
1 teaspoon salt
½ cup shortening
Enough ice water to barely
mix

Note: There are many recipes for pastry, but this one is the one that I learned in college and I still like it. It is better if you chill it before you roll it out. Try not to handle dough much and always roll away from you.

Cream Cheese Pastry

1 cup butter
1 cup cream cheese
¼ cup heavy cream
2½ cups flour
1 teaspoon salt

Mix all ingredients and chill well before rolling pastry out.

P.S. You can use this for tart shells or for making hors d'oeuvres. I frequently cut it in small rounds and fold them over a filling, such as anchovy paste. You can make up lots of combinations for the fillings for hors d'oeuvres or tarts.

Pastry Cream

2 tablespoons flour
1 cup light cream
⅛ teaspoon salt
⅜ cup sugar
4 egg yolks
2 teaspoons vanilla

Combine flour with ¼ cup cream and stir until smooth. Gradually add remaining cream. Put in saucepan and stir in salt and sugar. Cook over medium heat, stirring until it thickens. Stir a small amount into beaten egg yolks. Return mixture to pan, stirring hard. Add vanilla. Cook over low heat and let thicken a little more. *Do not boil.* Cool quickly.

P.S. You can use this as a filling for cream puffs or flavor and use as a filling for small tarts. I usually make this with the four egg yolks left when I make meringues. If you keep this in the "fridge", cover it with plastic wrap.

Tiny Almond Pies

1 recipe Rich Pastry
½ cup raspberry preserves
2 egg yolks
½ cup sugar
6 tablespoons ground almonds
1 tablespoon flour
2½ teaspoons finely grated
   lemon rind
3 tablespoons heavy cream
¼ cup sliced almonds
2 tablespoons sugar

Grease small muffin tins (about 1¾″ in size) and line with pastry. Drop a little bit of the raspberry preserves in bottom of each pastry.

Beat together egg yolks, sugar, ground almonds, flour and lemon rind. Add cream and beat mixture until smooth. Spoon mixture into pastry, filling almost to the top. Place 2 slices of almond on top of each and sprinkle with sugar. Bake at 375° for about 20 minutes until golden brown. Allow to cool slightly before removing from pans.

P.S. These are my loves!

Apple Tarts

4 medium size apples
1 cup sugar
2 slices lemon
1 cup water
½ teaspoon salt
2 cinnamon sticks
6 tart shells, baked

Wash, peel and core apples. Cut in quarters and set aside. Combine next 5 ingredients in saucepan and bring to a boil. Add apples. Cover and cook 10 minutes, stirring carefully so as not to break apples. Remove from heat and allow to stand, covered, for 5 minutes. Remove apples. Boil syrup until thick. Pour over apples. Cool. Fill tart shells. Serve with whipped cream or hard sauce. Serves 6.

P.S. Get Granny Smith apples if possible.

167

Almond Pastry For Tarts

12 tablespoons butter
4 tablespoons sugar
1 teaspoon vanilla
Pinch of salt
2 cups flour (scant)
6 tablespoons powdered
  almonds
1 beaten egg

Put butter (broken into pieces), sugar, vanilla, salt, flour, and powdered almonds in food processor (or electric mixer), add egg, mix rapidly. Do not overwork. Wrap well and let stand in "fridge" 24 hours.

Roll your pastry and fit it into tart pans (I use small ones). Cover with parchment paper (cut to fit tart pans). Fill with lentils, dried beans or rice. Bake in 425° oven until pastry is light brown. (Remove lentils, etc., before completely done.) Allow tarts to cool and fill with one of the following fillings:

Note: Put slivered almonds in blender to make your powdered almonds.

Filling For Tarts

Lemon Cream:

1 cup milk
2 tablespoons sugar
3 egg yolks
3 tablespoons cornstarch
½ teaspoon vanilla
Juice of 3 lemons
Rind of 1 lemon, finely grated

Put milk in saucepan and bring to a boil. Cover and keep warm. Beat sugar and egg yolks until mixture thickens and forms a ribbon. Stir in cornstarch and slowly pour in some of hot milk (still beating). Pour mixture back in pan and stir constantly with wire whisk until thickened. Add vanilla, lemon juice and rind. Pour into bowl and cool. Add meringue on following page to filling.

Note: You can make variations of the filling. Leave out the lemon juice and rind and add 3 squares of melted semi-sweet chocolate while mixture is hot. Or caramelize about 4 or 5 tablespoons sugar and put into hot filling in place of lemon juice and rind. (When you put caramelized sugar into a mixture, be sure the mixture is very hot, otherwise the sugar will not blend in.) Or flavor filling with apricot brandy and add some apricot preserves— strawberries, peaches! Get the idea?

Italian Meringue:

3 egg whites
¾ cup sugar
3 tablespoons water

Beat egg whites until very firm, adding 1 tablespoon sugar during beating. Put remaining sugar and water in pan and boil until it reaches hard ball stage (248°). Pour cooked syrup *slowly* into beaten egg whites. Continue beating at low speed until mixture has cooled. Carefully fold ⅓ of meringue into lemon cream or other filling with wire whisk.

Put filling in tart shells and cover with remaining meringue. Sprinkle with powdered sugar and place under broiler until light brown.

P.S. Don't put your filling in too long before serving. I put the meringue for the top of the tarts in my pastry tube and use the star shaped tip to cover in little peaks. Pretty! This is a great recipe!

P.P.S. The pastry recipe makes about 20 tart shells and the filling recipe is for about 8 or 9 tarts. So I always have some shells left to freeze.

169

Rosette Wafers

2 eggs
1 tablespoon sugar
¼ teaspoon salt
1 cup flour
1 cup milk
Oil for frying

Beat eggs with sugar and salt. Add flour and milk alternately. Beat well.

Heat saucepan ½ full of oil. Dip rosette iron in hot oil then dip in batter just to the top of iron. Do not let batter come over top of iron. Submerge battered iron in oil until brown. This will take a little trial and error. When brown, slip off iron and cool.

Note: You can find the rosette irons at any kitchen supply counter in different shapes. These are fun to make and delicious with creamed chicken, etc., over them. I have the little Christmas tree irons and they make cute Christmas cookies sprinkled with powdered sugar and cinnamon.

Fudge Sundae Pie

1 cup evaporated milk
6 oz. semi-sweet chocolate
  chips
¼ teaspoon salt
1 cup miniature
  marshmallows
Grated pecans
1¼ cups vanilla wafers
½ cup melted butter
¼ cup sugar
1 quart vanilla ice cream

Combine milk, chocolate chips and salt in top of double boiler and cook until thick. Remove from stove and add marshmallows. Stir sauce until blended.

Make crust of vanilla wafers, butter and sugar. Alternate layers of ice cream and chocolate sauce. Top with grated pecans. Freeze. May be frozen in ice tray or pie tin.

P.S. When the grandchildren visit me, they always check the refrigerator to be sure I have some of this on hand.

Apple Cheese Pie À La Joan

Pastry:

3 oz. cream cheese
½ cup margarine
1½ cups sifted flour
1 tablespoon grated orange
  rind
1 tablespoon sugar
⅛ teaspoon salt
1 egg white

Combine all ingredients except egg white and mix with electric beater until well blended. Wrap in waxed paper and refrigerate at least 1 hour. Roll and put in pie pan. Brush with egg white and sprinkle with a little additional sugar. Bake at 350° for 15 minutes.

Filling:

4 large tart apples
½ cup sugar
½ cup orange juice
¼ cup sugar
1 tablespoon melted butter
1 teaspoon cornstarch
1 tablespoon lemon juice
1 tablespoon grated orange rind
Whipped cream

Peel and dice apples. Add ½ cup of sugar and steam on top of stove until transparent. Stir to keep from burning, but do not break apples. Mix other ingredients and pour over apples. Fill pastry and cook in oven until apples are tender. Top with whipped cream.

Fudge Pie

½ cup butter
3 oz. unsweetened chocolate
4 eggs
1½ cups sugar
3 tablespoons white corn
  syrup
¼ teaspoon salt
1 teaspoon vanilla
9″ pie shell, unbaked

In top of double boiler, melt butter and chocolate. Cool. Beat eggs until light and beat in sugar, corn syrup, salt and vanilla. Add chocolate mixture and mix thoroughly. Pour into unbaked pie shell. Bake at 350° for 25 minutes or until top is crusty and filling is somewhat soft inside. Do not overcook. Pie should have custard-like consistency. Top with whipped cream.

Note: Not good for the figure but great for the taste buds.

Baklava

1 lb. phyllo leaves
2 cups finely chopped pecans
1 cup finely chopped almonds
¾ cup sugar
1 teaspoon cinnamon
¼ teaspoon nutmeg
3 cups unsalted sweet butter

Preheat oven to 325°. If using frozen phyllo, allow to defrost in ice box before handling. Remove phyllo leaves from package, being careful to always keep them covered with wax paper and a damp cloth. Mix nuts, sugar, cinnamon and nutmeg. Place 2 pastry leaves in a 15x10x1" jellyroll pan. Brush top with melted butter. (I use a large pastry brush.) Continue stacking 10 more leaves, buttering every other leaf. Sprinkle with ⅓ of the nut mixture. Add 4 more leaves, buttering every other leaf. Sprinkle with ⅓ of nut mixture. Add 4 more leaves, buttering as usual. Add remaining nut mixture. Stack any remaining leaves. Butter top. Trim edges if necessary. With a sharp knife, cut through top layer on long side, making 8 diagonal cuts at 1½" intervals to form diamonds. (Cut through top layer only.) Bake 60 minutes at 325° or until golden brown. Turn off heat and leave in oven 60 minutes longer. Remove and pour following syrup over Baklava. Cut all the way through in diamonds and let cool on the pan. Makes about 35 pieces.

To make vanilla sugar, put several split vanilla beans in a jar of sugar and cover tightly —

Syrup:

¾ cup sugar
1½ cups honey
2 cinnamon sticks
4 lemon slices
4 orange slices
¾ cup water

Combine ingredients. Bring to a boil, cut down heat and simmer uncovered for 10 minutes. Strain and put aside to cool.

P.S. You have to work fast if you are using frozen phyllo. It is very difficult to handle and must be kept moist. The frozen phyllo I have bought is 22x18". Just trim edges to size I have given you. These are a lot of trouble and "sinfully" rich, but Oh! so good.

Deep Apple Pie

¾ cup sugar
2 tablespoons flour
1 cup sour cream
1 egg, well beaten
½ teaspoon vanilla
1 teaspoon salt
2 cups chopped apples
Pastry shell, uncooked

Combine sugar, flour, sour cream, egg, vanilla and salt. Beat until smooth. Add chopped apples and mix. Pour into uncooked pie shell that has been placed in a medium sized casserole. Cook at 450° for 15 minutes, then reduce heat 150°, continue to cook 30 minutes longer. Spread the following mixture over the top of pie and cook 20 minutes longer:

Topping:

½ cup sugar
½ cup flour
¼ cup butter
1 tablespoon cinnamon

P.S. This is my mother's recipe for apple pie, and my daughters were crazy about it when they were young. When they are not dieting, they still love it.

Great Grandmother Hampton's Chess Pie

½ cup butter
1 cup dark brown sugar
2 tablespoons granulated
   sugar
3 eggs
1 teaspoon vanilla
Juice of 1 medium lemon
Grated rind of 1 lemon
9″ pie shell, unbaked

Melt butter in medium sized saucepan, add sugar and simmer for a few minutes. Remove from heat, allow to cool slightly and beat in eggs, one at a time. Then add vanilla, lemon juice and rind. Mix well and pour into unbaked pie shell. Cook in 400° oven for 15 minutes. Reduce heat to 350° and continue baking for about 20 minutes more. Shake pie gently, pie is done when it quivers slightly.

P.S. Watch your crust and if it browns too soon, cover pie with a tent of aluminum foil until done. Serve warm with a spoonful of whipped cream or vanilla ice cream.

P.P.S. This is a very old recipe. My mother said it was her grandmother's recipe. Great grandmother Hampton was married in 1840 so the recipe goes back at least to the middle 1800's.

Mrs. Valentine's Chocolate Tarts

¾ cup sugar
1½ tablespoons cornstarch
1½ tablespoons cocoa
2 egg yolks
1½ cups milk
2 tablespoons margarine
1½ teaspoons vanilla
6 individual tart shells, baked
Whipped cream

Mix sugar, cornstarch and cocoa. Add beaten egg yolks and slowly add milk. Cook over low heat, stirring constantly until thickened. Add margarine and vanilla. Fill pie shells and serve topped with whipped cream.

P.S. These are easy to make and taste like brown velvet. Better served when filling is warm.

Cherry Tarts

1 (16 oz.) can pie cherries
Sugar to taste
2 tablespoons cornstarch
4 slices lemon
2 tablespoons butter
Red food coloring
6 individual tart shells, baked

Put the cherries in saucepan, reserving about ½ of the juice. Sweeten to taste. Heat over medium heat. When the cherries come to a boil, add cornstarch which has been blended with reserved cherry juice, and add slices of lemon. Let boil gently until thickened, stirring with a fork to keep from tearing up the cherries. When thickened, add butter and 1 drop of red food coloring. Discard lemon slices and serve warm in individual pie shells with either ice cream, whipped cream or hard sauce on top.

P.S. If you like the filling any thicker than this makes it, just add additional cornstarch. I can't tell you the amount of sugar as it will depend on how tart the cherries are. We like this better made with frozen cherries when we can get them.

Coconut Pie

½ cup butter, softened
1½ cups sugar (scant)
3 eggs
1 tablespoon white vinegar
1 teaspoon vanilla
1 cup coconut
9″ pie shell, unbaked

Cream butter and sugar together. Add the eggs one at a time, beating well after each addition. Blend in well the vinegar, vanilla and coconut. Put in pie shell and bake at 325° for 1 hour.

P.S. Use either fresh grated coconut or frozen grated coconut. If you like coconut pie, this is the best. And I am allergic to it, darn it!

Bittersweet Chocolate Mint Pie

½ cup sugar
1 envelope gelatine
1 tablespoon cornstarch
1 cup milk
3 egg yolks
1 square unsweetened
chocolate
⅓ cup green crème de menthe
Few drops green coloring
3 egg whites
¼ cup sugar
½ cup whipping cream
9″ pie shell, baked

In saucepan combine ½ cup sugar, gelatine and cornstarch. Slowly stir in the milk. Cook and stir until gelatine is dissolved. Beat egg yolks slightly, stir in some of the hot mixture and return all to pan. Cook for 2 minutes more. Divide mixture into two portions.

To one portion add chocolate that has been melted and cooled. Chill this until it will mound when stirred. Stir the crème de menthe into the remaining mixture, add the coloring and chill until thickened.

Meanwhile, beat egg whites until stiff and gradually add ¼ cup sugar. Whip cream and fold it into the egg whites with a wire whisk. Mix one half with the chilled chocolate mixture and the other half with the crème de menthe mixture. Pour the chocolate mixture into the pie shell and chill for 30 minutes. When chilled, spoon the crème de menthe mixture over the chocolate and chill overnight.

P.S. I serve this with some whipped cream on top. If you are dieting, grate some chocolate on top instead.

Always chill your bowl before whipping cream —

Black Bottom Pie

5 tablespoons melted butter
14 ginger snaps, rolled fine
1½ squares unsweetened
   chocolate
2 cups scalded milk
1 cup sugar
1½ tablespoons cornstarch
4 egg yolks, well beaten
1 teaspoon vanilla
1 tablespoon gelatine
2 tablespoons water
4 egg whites, beaten
½ teaspoon cream of tartar
2 tablespoons whiskey
½ pint cream, whipped
Grated unsweetened
   chocolate

Add melted butter to ginger snap crumbs. Mix well and line pie pan. Bake at 400° for 10 minutes, remove from oven and set aside. Melt chocolate in saucepan and set aside. Make a custard out of the scalded milk, ½ cup sugar, cornstarch and well beaten egg yolks. Cook until custard coats a spoon. Take out 1 cup of custard, add to it the melted chocolate and add vanilla. Cool and put in pie shell. Mix gelatine and water. Add to remainder of hot custard. Cool. Beat egg whites until frothy and add cream of tartar and ½ cup sugar and continue beating until stiff. Fold into custard and add whiskey. Pour into pie shell. Spread whipped cream over mixture and grate chocolate over top of cream.

P.S. This makes a big beautiful pie and is not too much trouble. (That's not really true, it is trouble but worth it.)

Japanese Fruit Pie

½ cup butter
1 cup sugar
2 eggs
1 tablespoon vinegar
½ cup sweetened coconut
½ cup golden raisins
½ cup chopped pecans
9″ pie shell, unbaked

Mix ingredients and place in pie shell. Bake at 325° for 40 minutes.

Cream Puffs

½ cup butter
1 cup water
1 cup sifted flour
¼ teaspoon salt
4 eggs

Combine butter and water in a saucepan. Cook over medium heat until butter is melted and mixture is boiling. Turn heat very low, add flour and salt, all at one time. Stir until a ball forms in middle of pan. Remove from heat, add 3 of the eggs, one at a time, and beat hard and long after each addition. Final egg should be beaten lightly with fork and added gradually. Put spoonfuls on cookie sheet. Bake at 375° until golden brown and no moisture shows. Stick point of small knife in side of each puff. Turn heat off and leave in oven about 10-15 minutes more.

Note: The steam evaporates and they are not soggy if baked this way. Fill with any cream filling or chocolate filling. They are easy to make. You can fill them using a pastry tube or just make a hole and put the filling in. Melt semi-sweet chocolate and glaze some of them, or add a little whipped cream to the top.

Pecan Pie

1 cup sugar
½ cup dark corn syrup
4 tablespoons butter
3 eggs, beaten
1 teaspoon vanilla
Dash salt
1 cup broken pecans
9″ pie shell, unbaked

Combine sugar, corn syrup, and butter in small saucepan. Bring to a boil. Remove from heat and stir in the eggs, well beaten. Add vanilla, salt and pecans, stirring until pecans are well coated. Pour into pie shell and bake at 375° for 35 or 40 minutes.

Pearl's Strudel

8 oz. cream cheese
1 cup butter (do not
  substitute)
2 cups flour
Apricot, strawberry or
  raspberry preserves
1 egg white
2 cups finely chopped pecans
Brown sugar

Have cream cheese and butter at room temperature. Cream and add flour. Divide dough into 3 balls and refrigerate at least 12 hours. Flour board and roll 1 ball of dough into rectangle (as thin as can be well handled). Spread carefully to within 1″ of the sides of the rectangle with preserves (not too thick). Sprinkle with brown sugar and ⅓ of the pecans. Starting with wide side, roll as for jelly roll. Seal edges with egg white and place seam side down on cookie sheet. Repeat with other two balls of dough using a different preserve with each. Bake in 300° oven until golden brown. Ice while still hot and on cookie sheet. Cut into small triangles when cool.

Icing:

1 cup powdered sugar
Juice of 1 lemon
Grated rind of 1 lemon

Mix and pour over strudel.

P.S. You can bake one roll and leave the other balls of dough in the ice box for several days. These are rich but Oh, so good!

Little Fellow Lemon Pies

½ cup butter
2 cups sugar
4 eggs
1 tablespoon flour
⅓ cup lemon juice
Pastry

Cream butter and sugar. Add eggs singly, beating until blended after each addition. Add flour, mix well. Stir in lemon juice. Line small muffin pans with pastry, fill each ⅔ full with lemon mixture. Bake at 350° for 30 minutes. Makes about 4 dozen small pies.

Note: These are just yummy!

179

Pear Tart

4 firm pears 2 cups dry red wine 1 cup water 2½ cups sugar	Peel, halve and core the pears. Combine other ingredients and bring to a boil. Drop pears into mixture, turn heat very low and slowly poach the pears until tender. Depending on firmness of pears, this can take over an hour. Pears should be tender but not soft. Remove after poaching and put aside to cool.

Pastry:

1½ cups flour
½ cup butter
3 tablespoons vegetable
  shortening
2 tablespoons sugar
¼ teaspoon salt
⅓ cup ice water

Blend flour, butter and vegetable shortening until like coarse meal. Dissolve sugar and salt in ice water and sprinkle over flour mixture to blend. Gather into a ball and wrap in waxed paper and chill thoroughly. Roll to ½″ thickness and line 9″ pie pan. Prick pastry with fork, cover with aluminum foil, and spread 1 cup of rice over the foil to prevent bubbling of crust. After 5 minutes in 425° oven, remove aluminum foil and rice. Prick crust again and bake until golden. Cool.

Cream Filling:

3 egg yolks
¼ cup sugar
¼ cup flour
1 cup hot milk
1 tablespoon butter
1 tablespoon vanilla

Beat egg yolks, add sugar and flour gradually and continue to beat until mixture ribbons. Add hot milk in thin stream beating continuously. Cook over moderate heat. When thickened, add butter and vanilla and set aside. To prevent formation of crust, sprinkle with 1 teaspoon of milk or rum.

Raspberry Glaze:

1 cup raspberry (or apricot) jelly
2 tablespoons sugar

Boil jelly and sugar together until candy thermometer reads 230° or mixture spins a thread. Cool.

To assemble, using pastry brush cover pastry shell with raspberry glaze. Pour in the cream filling and place pears decoratively over this base. Coat each pear with the following chocolate glaze. Decorate with toasted slivered almonds. Refrigerate until cream filling and chocolate glaze have set.

Chocolate Glaze:

4 squares semi-sweet chocolate
1 tablespoon butter

Melt over low heat.

P.S. This is a fantastic dessert that Bill and I spent a wonderful afternoon working out.

Dream Tarts

Pastry:

1 cup butter
3 oz. cream cheese
1 cup flour

Mix and press into small tart pans.

Filling:

¼ cup butter
1 cup sugar
2 eggs
1 cup golden raisins
1 cup chopped nuts
½ teaspoon vanilla

Cream butter with sugar. Add eggs, raisins, nuts and vanilla. Fill shells ¾ full and bake at 350° until brown.

Note: Good, but hard to get out of shells. They freeze well.

Chocolate Chiffon Pie

4 oz. unsweetened chocolate
1 envelope gelatine
1 cup sugar
4 eggs, separated
1 teaspoon vanilla
9″ pie shell, baked
Whipped cream
Grated chocolate

Melt chocolate in ½ cup water. Cool slightly. Soften gelatine in ¼ cup cold water, then add to the chocolate mixture and stir until gelatine is dissolved. Mix ½ cup sugar with egg yolks and combine with chocolate mixture. Add vanilla. Beat egg whites stiff with ½ cup sugar, fold into chocolate mixture which has been thoroughly cooled. Pour into cooked shell and chill at least 2 hours. Serve with whipped cream and grate unsweetened chocolate over the cream.

P.S. It's the easiest good pie I've ever made.

Chocolate Pie

1 cup sugar
5 tablespoons flour
4 tablespoons cocoa
3 egg yolks
2 cups milk
1 teaspoon vanilla
2 tablespoons butter
9″ pie shell, baked

Mix sugar, flour, and cocoa together. Add egg yolks and then gradually add milk, stirring. Mix well and cook in double boiler until thick. Remove from stove and add vanilla and butter. Pour filling into pie shell. Cover with following meringue and cook in 350° oven until meringue is brown.

Meringue:

3 egg whites
½ teaspoon cream of tartar
6 tablespoons sugar

Beat egg whites until frothy. Add cream of tartar. Slowly add sugar and continue to beat until thick and glossy.

Grasshopper Pie

1¼ cups rolled chocolate
  wafers
½ cup melted butter
20 large marshmallows
½ cup milk
1 cup heavy cream
3 tablespoons green crème
  de menthe
3 tablespoons white crème
  de cacao

Combine crushed wafers with the melted butter. Press into bottom and sides of pie pan. Chill. Melt marshmallows in the milk in top of double boiler. Cool. Whip cream and add the liqueurs. Fold into marshmallow mixture and pour into crust. Chill until firm.

*P.S. This is green, pretty and very light. Be sure to use **white** crème de cacao!*

Toasted Coconut Pie

4 egg yolks
5 tablespoons sugar
⅓ cup milk
1 package unflavored gelatine
2 teaspoons vanilla
4 egg whites
⅛ teaspoon salt
½ teaspoon cream of tartar
3 tablespoons sugar
1 cup cream, whipped
4 tablespoons Cognac
9″ pie shell, baked
2 teaspoons apricot glaze
1¾ cups shredded fresh
  coconut

Put egg yolks and sugar in top of double boiler. Beat with electric beater or wire whisk until lemon colored. Set over simmering water. Cook 5 minutes stirring constantly. Add milk and gelatine. Stir until gelatine is completely dissolved. Remove from heat, pour in large bowl, add vanilla and cool. Beat egg whites, salt and cream of tartar. Add sugar and beat until stiff. Fold into yolk mixture. Whip cream until soft peaks form. Add Cognac and beat until stiff. Add to mixture.

Paint crust with apricot glaze, spoon in filling and refrigerate until firm. Preheat oven to 350°. Spread coconut on cookie sheet and bake 5 or 6 minutes until lightly brown. Sprinkle coconut over pie.

Hawaiian Macadamia Nut Cream Pie

½ cup sugar
4½ tablespoons cornstarch
¼ teaspoon salt
2 cups milk
4 egg yolks, beaten
1 tablespoon butter
2 tablespoons coffee liqueur
¾ cup macadamia nuts,
   chopped
2 cups heavy cream, whipped
9″ pastry shell, baked

Combine sugar, cornstarch and salt in top of double boiler. Slowly add milk, stirring well. Place over hot water and cook until thickened to custard consistency. Blend hot mixture into beaten egg yolks 1 tablespoon at a time. Put mixture back into boiler and continue cooking until quite thick. Add butter and cool. When cool, stir in liqueur and macadamia nuts (reserving some for top). Fold in ¾ of whipped cream. Fill pastry shell. Garnish with rest of whipped cream and reserved nuts.

P.S. This reminds me of one fantastic trip to Hawaii with my daughters. That's where I found the recipe. It always brings back memories.

Toffee Pie

Vanilla wafers
Vanilla ice cream
1 cup crushed toffee bars
1 cup slivered almonds,
   toasted

Line a 7x11″ pan with vanilla wafers. Cover with a layer of ice cream. Sprinkle with the crushed toffee bars and the slivered almonds. Cover with another layer of ice cream. Freeze. To serve, cut the pie in squares and pour following sauce over.

Sauce:

1½ cups sugar
¼ cup white corn syrup
1 cup crushed toffee bars
½ stick margarine

Combine ingredients in saucepan and bring to a boil. Stir constantly until toffee melts.

P.S. Better if served when sauce is hot.

Cakes

Caramel Icing

3 cups sugar
1 cup milk
3 tablespoons sugar
¼ cup butter

Put sugar and milk in large saucepan and bring to a boil. Meantime, in skillet, caramelize 3 tablespoons sugar until it is brown. When milk-sugar mixture comes to a rolling boil, add the caramelized sugar, stirring all of the time. Cook until it will make a soft ball when dropped in cup of cold water. Have a soft ball that you can pick up and test in your fingers. Take off the stove and add butter and beat until icing is ready to spread on cake.

Note: Be careful when you pour caramelized sugar into milk mixture for it will boil and splatter all over you! This is the reason I said use a large boiler for this icing. It takes a lot of beating to make this creamy and spreadable, but it is worth it.

White Icing

1 cup sugar
⅓ cup water
⅛ teaspoon cream of tartar
Few grains salt
2 egg whites, stiffly beaten
1 teaspoon flavoring of choice

Cook sugar, water, cream of tartar and salt until it spins a long thread or until it reaches 240° on candy thermometer. Pour very slowly over stiffly beaten egg whites and continue beating until ready to spread.

Note: If you cook this syrup slowly and cover it the first few minutes so that it won't crystalize on sides of pan, the icing will be creamier.

Chocolate Filling

1½ cups sugar
¼ teaspoon cream of tartar
⅓ cup water
3 egg whites, beaten stiff
Pinch of salt
12 oz. semi-sweet chocolate
1 cup strong coffee
1 tablespoon vanilla
3 tablespoons rum
3 tablespoons cocoa
¼ cup butter

Put sugar, cream of tartar and water in a saucepan and boil until it forms a soft ball in cold water (238° on candy thermometer). Pour very slowly into the egg whites that have been beaten stiff with a pinch of salt. Beat with electric beater until cool (8 to 10 minutes) and set this meringue mixture aside.

Melt the chocolate with the coffee in top of double boiler. Add vanilla and rum to chocolate. Add cocoa and cool thoroughly. Soften butter and whip into meringue mixture. When chocolate is cool and stiff, fold into meringue.

Note: This is a heavenly chocolate filling! I use it for chocolate roll, the filling for cream puffs or to frost cakes. It never gets hard, you can eat it with a fork, and it is delicious. Try cutting an angel food cake into 3 layers. Put this between the layers and frost the cake with it. GOOD!!

Melt chocolate in slow oven on shaped aluminum foil. Scrape off with rubber spatula —

One Minute Icing

1 cup sugar
½ stick butter
¼ cup milk
2 tablespoons marshmallow
   cream
1 teaspoon vanilla

Mix sugar and butter and milk in saucepan and put over moderate heat. Stir constantly and when it comes to a boil, time exactly for 1 minute. Take from fire, add marshmallow cream and beat until thick enough to spread. It will be shiny. Add vanilla. Be strong, for this takes a little beating!

P.S. This is the classic "One Minute Icing." Add 4 tablespoons cocoa to make a chocolate icing or any other flavoring that strikes your fancy.

Mrs. Arnold's Fudge Cake

2 cups flour
1 teaspoon salt
2 cups sugar
½ cup margarine
1 cup water
½ cup oil
3 tablespoons cocoa
2 eggs
1 teaspoon soda
½ cup buttermilk
1 teaspoon vanilla

Put flour, salt and sugar in big mixing bowl. Mix margarine, water, oil and cocoa in saucepan and bring to a boil. Pour over flour, mix and beat well. Beat eggs and add soda, buttermilk and vanilla. Add to above mixture and beat well. Bake in greased floured pan 11x15" at 350° for 25-30 minutes. While cake is hot, pour warm icing over it.

Icing:

½ cup margarine
3 tablespoons cocoa
6 tablespoons evaporated milk
1 box powdered sugar
1 teaspoon vanilla
½ cup chopped nuts

Mix margarine, cocoa and milk and heat over low heat until margarine melts. Mix in sugar and beat. Add vanilla and nuts. Keep warm and spread over cake as soon as cake is done. Makes 40 squares.

P.S. Really good

Applesauce Muffin Cakes

1 cup butter
2 cups sugar
2 eggs
4 cups flour
1 teaspoon cinnamon
1 teaspoon allspice
2 teaspoons soda
2 cups applesauce
2 teaspoons vanilla

Cream butter and sugar and add eggs. Sift flour, cinnamon, allspice and soda. Add flour and applesauce alternately. Add vanilla. Pour into greased muffin tins and bake at 350° for about 10 minutes. Dust with powdered sugar.

P.S. I usually bake these in paper baking cups.

Caramel Pound Cake

1 cup butter
½ cup vegetable shortening
1 cup white sugar
1 lb. dark brown sugar
5 whole eggs
3 cups flour
½ teaspoon baking powder
¼ teaspoon salt
1 cup milk less 2 tablespoons
1 teaspoon vanilla
2 tablespoons coffee liqueur

Cream butter and shortening with white and brown sugars. Beat well. Add eggs one at a time. Add flour, baking powder, salt and milk alternately. Then add vanilla and coffee liqueur. Bake in 11" stem pan in 325° oven for about 1 hour and 15 minutes.

Icing:

1 cup sugar
1 cup light brown sugar
½ cup butter
½ cup milk

Combine sugars with butter and milk over moderate heat. Boil for 1 minute. Beat until ready to spread.

P.S. This is quite different from most pound cakes and keeps very well.

Carrot Cake

2 cups sugar
1½ cups salad oil
4 eggs
2 cups flour
2 teaspoons soda
3 teaspoons cinnamon
1 teaspoon salt
2 teaspoons vanilla
3 cups grated carrots

Combine sugar and oil. Beat in eggs until smooth. Add flour that has been sifted with soda, cinnamon and salt. Add vanilla and carrots. Pour into 3 greased and floured layer pans and bake at 325-350° for 30 minutes.

Icing:

½ cup margarine, softened
8 oz. cream cheese
1 lb. powdered sugar
1 cup chopped pecans
1 teaspoon vanilla (optional)

Mix together and spread over layers.

P.S. Olivia, this is for you.

Chocolate Muffin Cakes

4 oz. semi-sweet chocolate
2 sticks butter or margarine
1¾ cups sugar
Pinch of salt
1 cup flour
4 eggs
1 teaspoon vanilla
2 cups chopped pecans

Melt chocolate in top of double boiler with butter. Put in bowl and add sugar and salt. Stir well, add flour and eggs one at a time. Beat enough to mix; add vanilla and nuts. Bake at 325° for 25 minutes in muffin pans.

P.S. I use the paper baking cups for these. They taste very much like fudge cake. The kids will love them.

Chocolate Sundae Cake

6 oz. German chocolate
3 tablespoons water
3 tablespoons light cream
4 cups flour
1½ teaspoons baking powder
1½ teaspoons salt
¾ cup butter or margarine
¾ cup shortening
2¼ cups sugar
6 eggs
1½ cups milk
1½ teaspoons vanilla

Chocolate Glaze:

6 oz. German chocolate
2 teaspoons vegetable
   shortening

Grease, then flour 11″ tube pan. In double boiler (with hot water, not boiling), melt chocolate with water until smooth. Blend in cream. Sift together flour, baking powder and salt. At medium speed on mixer, cream butter with shortening, and gradually add sugar, beating at least 5 minutes. Beat in eggs, one at a time, beating 1 minute after each addition. Combine milk and vanilla. At low speed add sifted dry ingredients alternately with milk, beginning and ending with dry ingredients. Beat thoroughly after each addition. Pour about ¼ of batter in tube pan, then drizzle with about ⅓ of melted chocolate. Repeat with 2 or more layers with chocolate on top. Bake at 350° for 70-80 minutes. Cool 15 minutes, then remove from pan. When cake is cool, spoon on following chocolate glaze.

In double boiler, melt chocolate with vegetable shortening, stirring until smooth. Drizzle along top edge of cake.

P.S. This is a big beautiful cake!

191

Chocolate Pound Cake

1 cup butter or margarine
½ cup shortening
3 cups sugar
5 eggs
3 cups flour
½ tablespoon baking powder
½ teaspoon salt
4 tablespoons cocoa, heaping
1 cup milk
1 teaspoon vanilla

Cream butter, shortening and sugar. Add eggs and stir until blended. Sift dry ingredients together and add alternately with milk. Add vanilla. Bake in stem pan at 325° for 1 hour and 20 minutes.

P.S. I like this pound cake because it is not too sweet. It keeps well.

German Chocolate Cake

4 oz. German sweet chocolate
½ cup boiling water
1 cup butter
2 cups sugar
4 egg yolks
1 teaspoon vanilla
2½ cups sifted cake flour
½ teaspoon salt
1 teaspoon soda
1 cup buttermilk
4 egg whites

Melt chocolate in boiling water. Cool. Cream butter and sugar until light, add egg yolks, one at a time and beat well after each addition. Add melted chocolate and vanilla. Mix well. Sift together flour, salt and soda. Add alternately with buttermilk to chocolate mixture. Beat well. Beat egg whites stiff and fold into batter. Pour into three 8" or 9" layer pans lined with paper and buttered well. Bake at 350° for 25-30 minutes.

Frosting:

1 cup evaporated milk
1 cup sugar
¼ lb. margarine
3 egg yolks
1 teaspoon vanilla
1⅓ cups coconut
1 cup pecans, chopped

Combine milk, sugar, margarine, egg yolks and vanilla. Cook over medium heat, stirring constantly, until thickened (about 12 minutes). Add coconut and pecans. Beat until thick enough to spread.

P.S. Too "gooey" for me but most people like it.

Cranberry Upside Down Cake

9 tablespoons butter, softened
1 cup sugar
1 package fresh cranberries
1 large egg
1 teaspoon vanilla
1 teaspoon grated orange rind
1¼ cups flour
1½ teaspoons baking powder
¼ teaspoon salt
⅔ cup milk
⅓ cup red currant jelly
½ cup heavy cream, whipped
  (optional)

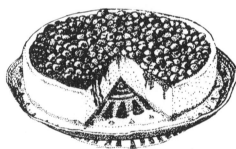

Butter the bottom and sides of 9″ round cake pan with 3 tablespoons soft butter. Sprinkle ½ cup sugar over bottom. Arrange washed and dried cranberries in pan.

In bowl, cream remaining butter and sugar. Add egg, vanilla and grated orange rind. Beat until well mixed. In another bowl, sift flour, baking powder and salt. Stir into butter mixture ½ cup at a time, alternating with milk. Stir until just combined. Pour batter over cranberries, smooth top and bake on a baking sheet in middle of oven preheated to 350° for 1 hour. Remove from oven and transfer to rack. Cool in pan for 20 minutes. Invert to cake stand. In small pan, melt jelly over low heat; brush over top of cake. Serve at room temperature with sweetened whipped cream, if desired.

Gingerbread

¼ cup butter
¼ cup sugar
1 beaten egg
½ cup molasses (or maple
  syrup)
¾ cup flour
1 teaspoon cloves
½ teaspoon soda
2 teaspoons cinnamon
1 teaspoon ginger
½ teaspoon salt
½ teaspoon baking soda
½ cup sour milk

Cream butter and sugar. Add beaten egg and molasses and beat for 1 minute. Sift dry ingredients together and add alternately with milk. Bake at 350° in a greased loaf pan or biscuit pan. Serve warm with ice cream or whipped cream.

P.S. No one could ever make this taste like Henrietta's gingerbread until one day she happened to say, "Of course we use maple syrup".

193

Cinnamon Coffee Cake

1 cup margarine
2 cups sugar
2 eggs
2 cups sifted flour
1 teaspoon baking powder
¼ teaspoon salt
1 cup sour cream
½ teaspoon vanilla

Cream margarine and sugar. Add eggs one at a time and stir until combined. Sift together flour, baking powder and salt. Add to egg mixture alternately with sour cream. Add vanilla. Pour into small angel food cake pan and add topping. Bake at 350° until done.

Topping:

¾ cup chopped nuts
1 teaspoon cinnamon
2 tablespoons brown sugar

Note: This is nice to serve for a morning coffee or a Coke party.

Strudel Filled Coffee Cake

1½ cups flour
3 teaspoons baking powder
¾ cup sugar
¼ teaspoon salt
¼ cup shortening
1 egg
½ cup milk
1 teaspoon vanilla

Sift flour, baking powder, sugar and salt together. Cut in shortening until like cornmeal. Blend in well beaten egg mixed with milk. Add vanilla and beat enough to stir. Pour ½ of the batter into well greased and floured 6x10″ heavy pan. Sprinkle with ½ of strudel mixture. Add remaining batter, sprinkle rest of strudel mixture on top. Bake in 375° oven for 25 to 30 minutes.

Strudel Mixture:

½ cup brown sugar
2 tablespoons flour
2 tablespoons cinnamon
2 tablespoons melted butter
½ cup chopped nuts

Mix dry ingredients, blend in melted butter and nuts. Mix well.

Note: This is the coffee cake I whipped up for our afternoon tea parties. You can double this recipe and bake in an angel food cake pan.

194

Devil's Food Cake

¾ cup butter
1½ cups sugar
3 egg yolks, beaten
2 oz. unsweetened chocolate
⅓ cup water
1⅓ cups flour
2 teaspoons baking powder
Pinch of salt
¾ cup milk
½ teaspoon almond flavoring
1 teaspoon vanilla
5 egg whites, beaten

Angel Icing:

1½ cups sugar
⅔ cup water
⅔ teaspoon cream of tartar
4 egg whites, beaten
1 teaspoon vanilla
½ teaspoon almond flavoring

Cream butter and sugar, add beaten egg yolks. Melt chocolate with water and cool slightly. Add to butter mixture. Add dry ingredients which have been sifted together, alternately with milk, beginning and ending with dry ingredients. Add flavorings and fold in well beaten egg whites. Pour into two well buttered 9″ cake pans and bake at 375° for about 25 minutes. Test and do not overcook. I suggest the following icing:

Put sugar, water and cream of tartar in saucepan. Heat and stir until sugar dissolves and mixture comes to a boil. Put lid on pan and cook 2 minutes so that sugar crystals on side of pan dissolve. Remove lid and cook until syrup reaches 242° on candy thermometer (that is medium ball stage). Pour syrup slowly into stiffly beaten egg whites, add flavorings and continue to beat until thick and stiff.

P.S. This cake is an old recipe and is a really good chocolate cake. The angel icing never gets completely dry, is definitely "fork food" but is light and delicate. It is about the consistency of whipped cream.

P.P.S. I guess the combination of Devil's Food Cake and Angel Icing sort of intrigues me.

Fudge Cake Henrietta Grayer

½ cup butter
1 cup sugar
⅔ cup flour
2 eggs
1 cup chopped pecans
3 tablespoons cocoa
1 teaspoon vanilla

Combine all ingredients. Beat well and pour into 9″ square cake pan that has been lined with greased brown paper. Bake at 250°. Usually takes about 40 minutes to bake, but you will have to be the judge and test it. Do not overcook. Ice with Chocolate One Minute Icing.

Chocolate One Minute Icing:

1 cup sugar
¼ cup butter
¼ cup milk
4 tablespoons cocoa
2 tablespoons marshmallow
  cream
1 teaspoon vanilla

Mix sugar, butter, cocoa, milk, in saucepan and put over moderate heat. Stir constantly and when it comes to a boil, time exactly for 1 minute. Take from fire, add marshmallow cream and beat until thick enough to spread. It will be shiny. Add vanilla. Be strong, for this takes a little beating!

P.S. Nobody can make this like Henrietta does, but it is without question, the best fudge cake you have ever put in your mouth! Try it!

Lightning Chocolate Cake

2 oz. unsweetened chocolate
4 tablespoons butter
1 cup sugar
1 cup flour
2 teaspoons baking powder
2 eggs
½ cup (good measure) milk
1 tablespoon vanilla

Melt chocolate with butter. Add remaining ingredients. Beat several minutes and pour into shallow pan that has greased brown paper in the bottom. Bake at 350° until done. Frost with Chocolate One Minute Icing.

Note: This is just as easy as cake mix, and even cheaper. Just dump it all into a bowl and beat. It should be a thin batter.

White Cake

½ cup shortening
1½ cups sugar
2½ cups cake flour
1 cup milk
¼ teaspoon salt
2½ teaspoons baking powder
4 egg whites, stiffly beaten
1 teaspoon vanilla

Cream shortening and sugar thoroughly, add 2 cups of the flour alternately with milk. Sift salt and baking powder with remaining flour and add to mixture. Fold in egg whites and vanilla. Pour into two layer pans and bake in 350° oven until cake tester comes out clean.

P.S. This is the white cake Henrietta makes. She likes it better than any other recipe for white cake. We use the 70¢ spread for shortening.

P.S. It's $1.00 now!

P.P.S. Make it $1.50

P.P.P.S. $2.25 now. The common name is butter.

Orange Cakes

¼ cup butter
½ cup sugar
5 egg yolks
⅞ cup flour
1½ teaspoons baking powder
¼ cup milk or orange juice
1 teaspoon grated orange rind

Cream butter and sugar together until fluffy. Add beaten egg yolks and stir to combine well. Add sifted dry ingredients and milk or orange juice alternately. Add orange rind and pour into paper muffin cups that have been placed in muffin tins. Bake at 375° for 15-20 minutes or until done. Cool and spread tops with orange icing. Makes a good dozen.

Orange Icing:

3 tablespoons butter
1½ cups sifted powdered
   sugar
Orange juice
1 teaspoon grated orange peel

Mix butter and sugar together until smooth. Add orange juice until spreadable. Add orange peel.

Note: These keep very well.

Coconut Pound Cake

1 cup shortening
½ cup butter
2½ cups sugar
5 large eggs
3 cups sifted flour
1 teaspoon baking powder
½ teaspoon salt
1 cup milk
1 tablespoon coconut
   flavoring
3½ oz. flaked coconut

Mix shortening, butter and sugar until very light. Add eggs one at a time, beating well after each addition. Add dry ingredients mixing alternately with milk. Add coconut flavoring and coconut. Pour into 11" tube pan that has been greased and floured. Place in a cold oven and set at 325° and bake 1 hour and 25 minutes.

P.S. This is really a honey of a cake. Easy to make and fun to eat.

P.P.S. You must not substitute margarine for the stick of butter. You have to use the real article.

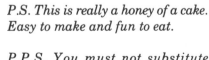

Lady Finger Cake

40 lady fingers, sprinkled with Grand Marnier
2 cups heavy cream, whipped
2¼ cups chopped macadamia nuts
Chocolate curls

Put 10 lady fingers in bottom of 8″ cake pan. Cover with ⅓ of following filling. Add lady fingers and cover with filling twice more. Finish with layer of lady fingers. Press down so cake will be formed. Refrigerate. Cover with whipped cream, chopped nuts and chocolate curls.

Filling:

½ lb. butter
5 egg yolks
½ cup sugar
2 tablespoons honey
1¼ oz. Grand Marnier
1 cup heavy cream, whipped
2¾ cups chopped macadamia nuts

Put butter in food processor and beat until light, add egg yolks one at a time, beating well. Blend sugar, honey and liqueur into mixture. Remove and fold in whipped cream and nuts. Do not overmix.

P.S. This is an adaptation of another recipe from Honolulu. This is rich, but who worries about calories?

White Fruit Cake

1½ cups butter
2 cups sugar
6 eggs
1 lb. candied pineapple
1 lb. pecans, chopped
4 cups flour
2 teaspoons baking powder
½ cup whiskey
2 teaspoons vanilla

Cream butter and sugar. Add eggs one at a time, mixing well after each addition. Dredge the pineapple and pecans in a few tablespoons of flour. Sift the remaining flour with baking powder. Mix with butter mixture and add candied pineapple, pecans, whiskey and vanilla. Mix well and bake in 250° oven for 2 to 2½ hours.

Note: You do not have to grease the pan, just flour it.

My Best Dark Fruit Cake

1 lb. orange peel, lemon peel
and citron
1 lb. pineapple
1 lb. candied cherries
½ gallon mixed nuts (pecans,
almonds and brazil nuts)
1 lb. butter
1 lb. sugar
10 eggs, separated
1 lb. flour
1 teaspoon baking powder
1 teaspoon nutmeg
1 tablespoon cinnamon
4 oz. Bourbon
1 pint strawberry preserves
1 pint fig preserves

Chop up all fruits and nuts, dredge with about ½ cup additional flour. Cream butter with sugar and beat in egg yolks. Stir in dry ingredients and Bourbon. Beat egg whites until they hold soft peaks and fold into mixture. Add fruits, nuts and preserves. Bake in well greased cake or loaf pans at 250° for about 2 hours. This makes several cakes.

Note: Don't forget, a little Bourbon sprinkled on top after it is baked and cooled, keeps it moist.

Dad's White Fruit Cake

½ lb. crystalized pineapple
½ lb. crystalized cherries
½ lb. crystalized orange peel
½ lb. white raisins
½ lb. green cherries
1 qt. pecans
2 cups flour
4 oz. whiskey
6 egg whites, beaten
½ teaspoon salt
1 teaspoon baking powder
1 cup sugar

Chop fruit and nuts, dredge in a little flour and pour whiskey over them. Beat egg whites and salt until very stiff, fold in remaining flour and baking powder which has been sifted together. Pour egg white mixture over fruit and mix. Bake in floured angel food cake pan at 250° for 3 hours.

P.S. Baste this cake with some of that mean old whiskey every few days. This does not keep as well as dark fruit cake.

P.P.S. No matter how many recipes I tried for dark fruit cake, it was not Christmas at our house until I made this cake.

Chocolate Macaroon Cake

Macaroon Mixture:

2 egg whites (reserve yolks
   for icing)
1 teaspoon vanilla
½ cup sugar
2 cups finely grated coconut
   (or 7 oz. package)
2 tablespoons flour

Beat egg whites with vanilla until stiff. Add sugar and beat until very stiff. Stir in coconut and flour. Set aside.

Chocolate Batter:

½ cup cocoa
¾ cup hot coffee
3 egg whites
1¾ cups sugar
1 teaspoon soda
½ cup sour cream
½ cup shortening
3 egg yolks
1 teaspoon salt
1 teaspoon vanilla
2 cups flour

Dissolve cocoa in hot coffee. Beat egg whites and add ½ cup sugar gradually. Add soda to sour cream. Beat 1¼ cups sugar with shortening, egg yolks, salt, vanilla and half the cocoa mixture until light and creamy (about 4 minutes). Add flour, the sour cream and remaining cocoa mixture. Blend well and fold in stiffly beaten egg whites.

Turn ⅓ of chocolate batter into a well greased 10" tube pan. Place half of macaroon mixture on top of this. Next add ½ of remaining chocolate mixture. Top with remaining macaroon mixture then remaining chocolate batter. Bake at 350° for 55-60 minutes. Cool completely before removing from pan.

Frosting:

6 oz. chocolate chips
2 tablespoons melted butter
2 egg yolks
1½ to 2 cups powdered sugar
½ cup sour cream
1 teaspoon vanilla

Melt chocolate chips in top of double boiler. Add melted butter, egg yolks, powdered sugar, sour cream and vanilla. Beat. Frost cake when cold.

P.S. Sounds like a lot of trouble, but it's worth it.

201

Nina's Cake

2½ cups flour
1 teaspoon soda
½ teaspoon salt
3 eggs
½ teaspoon lemon juice
1½ cups sour milk
1⅔ cups sugar
4 oz. German chocolate
½ cup butter
1 tablespoon vanilla

Sift 1 cup flour with soda and salt. Put aside. Beat 1 egg, add lemon juice, ½ cup sour milk and ⅔ cup sugar. Cook over medium heat for 2 minutes. Add chocolate and cook until thick. Cool. Cream butter with 1 cup sugar and 2 eggs. Add sifted dry ingredients alternately with remainder of sour milk and vanilla. Add cooled custard. Cook in large square pan at 350°.

Icing:

3 cups sugar
1 oz. unsweetened chocolate
½ cup milk
¼ cup white corn syrup
½ cup butter
1 teaspoon vanilla

Combine all ingredients except vanilla and boil for 3 minutes. Add vanilla and beat until ready to spread.

French Date Cake

1 cup sugar
½ cup butter
2 beaten eggs
2 cups flour
1 cup buttermilk
1 teaspoon soda
2 tablespoons coffee
½ lb. dates, chopped
1 cup chopped pecans
Grated rind of 2 oranges

Cream sugar and butter together. Add beaten eggs and alternately add flour and buttermilk. Add the soda that has been dissolved in the coffee, dates, pecans and orange rind. Pour into buttered oblong cake pan and bake at 350° until cake tester comes out clean. Pour glaze over cake while still hot. Cut in squares and serve with whipped cream.

Glaze:

1 cup sugar
Juice of 2 large oranges

Dissolve sugar in orange juice and pour over cake.

Marguerite's Pound Cake

1 cup butter
½ cup shortening or
  margarine
3 cups sugar
½ teaspoon salt
5 large eggs
3 cups flour
½ teaspoon baking powder
½ cup milk
½ cup evaporated milk
1 teaspoon rum flavoring
1 teaspoon vanilla
1 teaspoon almond extract

Cream butter, shortening, sugar and salt. Add eggs one at a time, beating after each addition. Sift flour and baking powder. Add dry ingredients and milk alternately. Add flavorings to batter. Bake in 11″ stem pan or bundt pan in 325° oven for 1½ hours or until done.

Toasted Butter Pecan Cake

2 cups chopped pecans
1¼ cups butter
3 cups flour
2 teaspoons baking powder
½ teaspoon salt
2 cups sugar
4 eggs, unbeaten
1 cup milk
2 tablespoons vanilla

Toast pecans in ¼ cup butter until brown. Sift flour with baking powder and salt (reserving about 2 tablespoons to dredge pecans with). Cream 1 cup butter and add sugar and eggs. Cream well. Add dry ingredients alternately with milk, beginning and ending with dry ingredients. Stir in vanilla and pecans. Cook in 3-9″ round layer pans, well greased. Bake at 350° for 25-30 minutes.

Butter Cream Frosting:

1 cup sugar
¼ cup water
⅛ teaspoon cream of tartar
⅛ teaspoon salt
2 egg whites
½ cup butter, softened
1 teaspoon vanilla

Combine sugar, water, cream of tartar and salt in saucepan. Bring to boil and cook until it forms a soft ball in cold water (240°). Beat egg whites stiff and slowly add syrup. Beat until stiff peaks form. Cool. When cool, add very soft butter, folding it in. Add vanilla and frost the cake.

Orange Wine Cake

½ cup butter
½ cup shortening
1½ cups sugar
4 eggs
3½ cups sifted flour
½ teaspoon salt
2 teaspoons baking soda
1½ cups buttermilk
1 cup finely chopped raisins
1 cup finely chopped pecans
2 teaspoons orange flavoring
2 tablespoons grated orange
   rind

Cream butter, shortening and sugar until light. Gradually add eggs. Then alternately add dry ingredients and buttermilk. Dredge raisins and nuts with ¼ cup of the flour. Add to mixture and add flavoring and orange rind. Pour into 2 greased 9″ round pans. Bake at 350° for 30 minutes. Frost with Sherry Frosting.

Sherry Frosting:

¼ cup butter
½ teaspoon orange flavoring
3 cups powdered sugar
Dash of salt
2½ teaspoons grated orange
   rind
¼ cup orange juice
Sherry

Mix ingredients and add sherry until right consistency to spread.

P.S. I always toast the pecans. This recipe calls for orange flavoring but I like to use 2 teaspoons frozen orange juice concentrate instead.

Nut Cake

¾ cup butter
2 cups sugar
6 egg yolks
½ cup molasses
¾ cup whiskey
4 cups sifted flour
½ teaspoon cloves
2 teaspoons cinnamon
½ teaspoon soda
1½ cups raisins
1 lb. chopped nuts
6 egg whites, stiffly beaten

Cream butter and sugar. Add egg yolks one at a time and beat well after each addition. Add molasses and whiskey. Add dry ingredients that have been sifted together, raisins and nuts. Add stiffly beaten egg whites. Pour into greased, buttered tube pan and bake at 275° until cake tester comes out clean.

P.S. This is an old recipe of my mother's and is delicious. In her day a cake tester was a broom straw.

Basic Sponge Sheet

4 eggs, separated
Pinch of salt
¼ cup sugar
½ teaspoon vanilla
6 tablespoons sifted
   cornstarch
6 tablespoons flour

Beat egg whites with salt until soft peaks form. Add sugar slowly and beat until very firm. Break egg yolks with fork, add vanilla. Fold ¼ of stiffly beaten whites thoroughly into yolks. Pour egg yolk mixture on top of remaining egg whites. Sprinkle cornstarch and flour over mixture and gently fold into whites until no pieces of egg white show. Don't overwork. Spread on a greased 11x16" jelly roll pan lined with waxed paper and greased again. Cook about 10 minutes at 400°. Trim edges and put on tea towel sprinkled with powdered sugar and roll immediately.

P.S. Try this with the chocolate filling, jelly or what you like, makes good petit fours, too.

Sour Cream Pound Cake

2 cups sugar
½ cup margarine
6 eggs
3 cups flour
¼ teaspoon salt
¼ teaspoon soda
1 cup sour cream
1 teaspoon vanilla
1 teaspoon lemon flavoring
¼ teaspoon almond flavoring

Cream sugar and margarine until light. Add eggs, one at a time, and beat well. Sift together dry ingredients and add alternately with sour cream. Add flavorings. Bake in tube or bundt pan at 325° for 1 hour. While hot, punch small holes in cake and pour over the following glaze:

Glaze:

¾ cup powdered sugar
1 tablespoon water
Juice of 1 lemon

Stir until dissolved.

Note: Easy and very light and good.

Sponge Cake

5 egg yolks
4½ teaspoons lemon juice
1½ teaspoons grated lemon
 rind
2 tablespoons water
5 egg whites
¼ teaspoon salt
¼ teaspoon cream of tartar
1 cup sugar
1 cup flour

Beat egg yolks until thick, add lemon juice, rind and water. Beat egg whites with salt and cream of tartar until stiff and dry. Gradually add sugar to yolk mixture and with wire whisk blend yolks into whites. Sift flour over egg mixture and blend in very gently. Bake in two ungreased 9″ pans in 350° oven for 25 minutes. Cool in pan and use spatula to remove.

P.S. This makes good ice cream cake. Soften 2 qts. of any good ice cream. Put a thick layer of ice cream between layers of cake and quickly ice cake with remaining ice cream. Freeze and serve slices with fresh fruit and whipped cream. Good to have in freezer for unexpected guests.

P.P.S. I remember one year when my grandson Kevin was little, I made this for his birthday and he asked for strawberries instead of candles. It was very pretty.

When heating egg whites be very sure your bowl is clean and dry.

Spiced Muffins

1 lb. raisins
1 cup butter
2 cups sugar
4 eggs
3½ cups flour
2 teaspoons allspice
1 teaspoon ground clove
2 teaspoons baking powder
2 teaspoons cinnamon
Powdered sugar

Cover raisins with about 1¼ cups of water and boil until raisins puff up. Pour off water, reserving 1 cup raisin water for use in the cakes. Cream butter and sugar and eggs. Add dry ingredients alternately with raisin water. One-half cup of the flour should be sprinkled over the raisins. Add raisins to cake mixture. Bake in paper baking cups in muffin tins. Sprinkle with powdered sugar when cool.

Note: These were commonly referred to as "fly" cakes when I was young.

Loaf Cake

1 cup butter or margarine
2 cups sugar
4 eggs
3½ cups cake flour
1 teaspoon salt
½ teaspoon soda
1 teaspoon baking powder
½ cup milk
½ cup buttermilk
1 teaspoon vanilla
1 teaspoon lemon extract

Cream butter and sugar well and add eggs. Beat 2½ minutes. Sift together cake flour, salt, soda and baking powder. Add to butter and sugar alternately with milk and buttermilk which have been mixed. Add vanilla and lemon extract. Bake in 10″ stem pan in 350° oven for about an hour.

Note: This cake may be iced with caramel, chocolate or your favorite icing (or it is good un-iced). I sometimes add 1 cup of chopped nuts to the batter and serve it without icing.

Orange Date Pound Cake

1 cup butter
2 cups sugar
4 eggs
1 teaspoon soda
1⅓ cups buttermilk
4 cups flour, sifted
2 teaspoons grated orange
  rind
1 lb. chopped dates
1 cup chopped pecans

Cream butter and sugar, add eggs one at a time, beat until smooth after each addition. Dissolve soda in buttermilk. Add sifted flour and buttermilk alternately in 3 parts. Add orange rind, dates and nuts. Mix well and pour into greased 11" stem pan. Cover pan with foil. Bake at 325° for 30 minutes. Remove foil and bake 1 hour more at same temperature. When done, pour sauce over cake and allow to cool in pan.

Sauce:

2 cups sugar
2 teaspoons grated orange
  rind
1 cup orange juice

Do not heat. Simply mix until sugar dissolves.

P.S. This cake keeps like a fruitcake and we think it is delicious. Punch small holes in cake and pour sauce over gradually while cake is still hot. It will finally absorb it all.

Red Velvet Cake

½ cup vegetable shortening
1½ cups sugar
2 whole eggs
2½ cups flour
1 teaspoon soda
2 tablespoons cocoa
1 teaspoon salt
1 cup buttermilk
1½ oz. red food coloring
2 tablespoons vanilla

Cream shortening and sugar. Add eggs and beat well. Sift dry ingredients together and add alternately with buttermilk. Add food coloring and vanilla. Bake in two round layer pans that have been greased and floured. Bake at 375° for 25 minutes or until cake tester comes out clean.

Frosting:

6 tablespoons flour
1 cup milk
1 cup butter
1 tablespoon vanilla
1 cup sugar

Mix flour and milk and cook in saucepan until very thick. Cool. Cream butter and sugar and add to cooled flour mixture. Beat until ready to frost. It takes a lot of beating.

P.S. How many birthday cakes I have made by this recipe in the more than 50 years since my first daughter was born! I've made at least a dozen just for Gigi.

White and Chocolate Cake

⅔ cup shortening
1⅔ cups sugar
2½ cups flour
1 tablespoon baking powder
1 teaspoon salt
3 eggs
1 teaspoon vanilla
1¼ cups milk

Cream shortening in mixing bowl with sugar, cream about 10 minutes. Sift flour, baking powder and salt several times. Add eggs to sugar and butter mixture, beating well after each addition. Add vanilla to milk. Add flour and milk alternately, at slow speed on mixer.

Chocolate Mixture:

1 tablespoon water
½ teaspoon almond extract
1½ tablespoons cocoa

Add water and almond extract to cocoa. Divide cake batter in two parts and add cocoa mixture to one half. Pour batters into two 9″ round cake pans that have been greased and floured. Preheat oven to 350° and bake cake for 30-35 minutes.

Frosting:

12 oz. semi-sweet chocolate
½ cup butter
2 cups powdered sugar
3 eggs
1 teaspoon vanilla

Melt chocolate. Blend butter and sugar in mixing bowl. Add eggs, one at a time. Add chocolate and vanilla. Beat until smooth and ready to spread.

Delicate Cake

White Cake:

¾ cup butter

2 cups sugar

3 cups flour

2 teaspoons baking powder

¾ cup milk

6 egg whites

1 teaspoon vanilla

1 teaspoon almond extract

½ teaspoon cinnamon

½ teaspoon nutmeg

¼ teaspoon allspice

Cream butter and sugar until fluffy. Sift together dry ingredients and add alternately with milk. Beat egg whites until stiff and fold into mixture. Add vanilla and almond extract. Divide the batter and reserve one half. To the other half of the batter add cinnamon, nutmeg, and allspice. This recipe makes two real thick layers or three medium layers. Bake in layer pans at 375° until tests done.

Cut up marshmallows, raisins, nuts, dates (if you like), red cherries, moistened with a little orange juice (not much) and a little grated orange rind added to make filling. Put the filling between the layers, and ice the cake with white icing.

P.S. This was my grandmother's recipe for cake. It was a favorite of Dad's and is another of our traditional Christmas cakes.

Cookies and Candy

Almond Chocolate Thins

1 cup butter
½ cup sugar
½ cup packed brown sugar
1 egg yolk
1 teaspoon vanilla
1¾ cups flour
1½ cups chopped almonds, roasted
6 oz. semi-sweet chocolate bits

Cream butter with both sugars. Beat in egg yolk and vanilla. Stir in flour and ½ cup almonds. Spread in 13x9″ pan. Bake at 350° for 20 minutes. Sprinkle with chocolate bits while hot. Spread over whole base as chocolate melts. Sprinkle with remaining ¾ cup almonds pressing them into chocolate. Cut into 1½″ squares while warm, but do not remove from pan until cold.

P.S. I like these - chocolate and almonds, what more do you want!

Chocolate Almond Butter Balls

1½ cups butter, softened
¾ cup sugar
1 egg yolk
1 teaspoon vanilla
½ teaspoon salt
3 oz. unsweetened chocolate
2 teaspoons grated orange rind
2 cups flour
1¼ cups finely chopped almonds

Cream butter with ½ cup of the sugar. Beat in egg yolk and salt. Melt 2 oz. of the chocolate and stir with orange rind into butter mixture. Add flour and ¾ cup almonds. Shape into 1½″ balls. Combine remaining ¼ cup sugar, 1 oz. chocolate and ½ cup chopped almonds in blender and process until blended. Roll balls in mixture. Bake on ungreased baking sheet at 350° for 13 minutes. Cool. Makes about 3 dozen.

Note: I always toast my almonds. I like them better that way.

Apricot Horns

Pastry:

½ lb. butter
2 cups flour
½ lb. creamed cottage cheese

Blend together in a mixing bowl. Shape into 1″ balls and refrigerate overnight.

Filling:

½ lb. dried apricots
1¼ cups sugar
2 tablespoons orange juice
2 tablespoons grated orange rind

Cook together until apricots are soft.

1 egg white
Powdered sugar
Chopped nuts

Roll the pastry balls and cut in 3″ circle with cookie cutter. Put a teaspoon of apricot mixture in center and roll into cornucopias. Brush with egg white (slightly beaten) and bake on greased cookie sheet at 375° for about 12 minutes. Dip in powdered sugar mixed with crushed nuts. Makes about 5 dozen.

P.S. This recipe calls for nuts, but I leave the nuts out of mine as I don't think they add much. Also, I like date filling better than apricot. Make it by cooking box of dates with orange juice and orange rind, mash well. Can also use prepared mincemeat.

Chinese Almond Cookies

2½ cups sifted flour
¾ cup sugar
¼ teaspoon salt
1 teaspoon baking powder
¾ cup soft shortening
1 egg
1 teaspoon almond extract
⅓ cup blanched almonds
1 egg yolk

Sift together flour, sugar, salt and baking powder. Mix shortening and egg until creamy. Add 2 tablespoons water and almond extract and mix. Gradually add flour mixture, stirring with fork until mixture draws away from sides of bowl. Knead to blend; chill 1 hour. Heat oven to 350°. Form dough into 1″ balls. Using palm of hand, flatten each to ¼″ thickness. Place on greased cookie sheet ½″ apart. Press almond in center of each. Brush with egg yolk beaten with 1 tablespoon water. Bake until golden, about 25 minutes.

P.S. These are among my favorites. They keep well.

Rocks

1 lb. dates
½ lb. candied cherries
½ lb. crystalized pineapple
1 lb. pecans
7 tablespoons whiskey
¾ cup butter
½ cup sugar
½ cup brown sugar
2 eggs
2 cups flour
1 tablespoon cinnamon
1 tablespoon nutmeg
1 tablespoon allspice
¾ teaspoon salt
1 teaspoon soda

Soak fruits and nuts in whiskey. Cream butter and sugars. Dissolve soda in 1 teaspoon boiling water. Add soda, eggs and sifted dry ingredients. Add whiskey soaked fruits and nuts. Mix well. Drop from a teaspoon on greased cookie sheet and bake at 325° for 15 minutes.

Note: This makes about 8 dozen cookies and they keep well. In fact, they are like fruit cake and are better about a week after you bake them.

Hello Dollies

½ cup butter or margarine
1½ cups graham cracker
   crumbs
1 cup coconut
1 cup semi-sweet chocolate
   bits
1 cup chopped pecans
1 (14 oz.) can Eagle Brand
   condensed milk

Melt butter in 7x11″ pan. Add graham cracker crumbs and pat into crust. Sprinkle the coconut over the crust. Over that sprinkle the chocolate bits, then cover with chopped pecans. Drizzle milk over the top. Bake at 350° for 25 minutes. Score into pieces while hot, but do not remove from pan until cold.

P.S. We all love these.

Madeleines

1½ cups sweet cream butter
4 eggs
1½ cups sugar
2 teaspoons finely grated
   lemon rind
1 teaspoon vanilla
2 cups flour

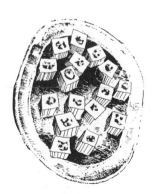

Melt butter and set aside to cool. Have eggs at room temperature. Mix eggs, sugar and lemon rind in large bowl. Place bowl over rim of wide pan containing 1 to 2 inches of water (not touching bowl). Place over low heat (do not boil), when egg mixture feels slightly warm to your finger, remove. Turn beater to high speed and beat until mixture is very light and has about tripled in bulk. Add vanilla and carefully fold in flour and finally the cooled butter. Fill well buttered madeleine pans about ⅔ full. Bake at 425° about 10 minutes or until light brown. Dust with powdered sugar. Makes about 3 dozen cookies.

P.S. If you have only one madeleine pan, be sure it is well buttered before each baking. These are light and delicious, however, you people who think "thin is beautiful" remember they are loaded with calories!

215

Lemon Squares

1 cup flour
6 tablespoons butter
2 eggs
1 cup brown sugar
½ cup chopped nuts
½ cup shredded coconut
½ teaspoon vanilla
⅛ teaspoon baking powder
1 teaspoon grated lemon rind
⅔ cup powdered sugar
1½ tablespoons lemon juice

Mix flour and butter, spread over 7x11" pan. Bake at 350° for 10 minutes. Mix eggs, brown sugar, nuts, coconut, vanilla, baking powder and lemon rind. Pour over cooked crust and bake until done. While still hot, combine powdered sugar and lemon juice and pour over top. Cool. Cut into squares to serve.

Note: You can tell to look at the brown sugar mixture when it is done. These are real yummy.

Sour Cream Cookies

½ cup butter
1 cup brown sugar
2 cups flour
1 egg
¾ cup sour cream
½ teaspoon soda
¼ teaspoon salt
1 tablespoon vanilla
2 oz. unsweetened chocolate
1 cup finely ground nuts

Mix and drop by teaspoon on greased cookie sheet. Bake at 350°.

Frosting:

¼ cup butter
2 tablespoons cocoa
Dash salt
2 teaspoons instant coffee
2 cups powdered sugar
2 tablespoons cream

Mix and spread over cookies.

Note: These are rich but yummy.

Cocoons

1 cup butter
2½ cups sifted flour
2 cups chopped nuts
6 tablespoons powdered sugar
½ teaspoon vanilla

Melt butter. Add flour, nuts, powdered sugar and vanilla. Work together and mold into little cocoons. Bake at 375° until light brown.

Note: A nice change is to leave the nuts and vanilla out, add ½ teaspoon almond extract and make into little round balls, indent center and put in either an almond, a candied cherry or a spoonful of strawberry or cherry preserves. They look pretty for a tea or a coffee.

P.S. Roll in powdered sugar and try not to eat too many!

Cheese Cake Cookies

⅓ cup brown sugar (packed)
½ cup chopped walnuts or
   pecans
1 cup flour
⅓ cup melted butter
1 tablespoon vanilla
8 oz. cream cheese
¼ cup sugar
1 egg
1 tablespoon lemon juice
2 tablespoons cream
1 teaspoon vanilla
Powdered sugar

Mix first 5 ingredients until about like meal. Reserving one cup of mixture, spread in an 8″ square cake pan (buttered). Bake at 350° for 12 minutes.

Put cream cheese in mixing bowl with sugar, egg, lemon juice, cream and vanilla. When well mixed, pour over cooked crust, sprinkle remaining crust mixture over top and bake for about 20-25 minutes. Cut in squares and sprinkle with powdered sugar.

Chinese Chews

½ cup butter
1 cup sugar
2 eggs, unbeaten
1 cup sifted flour
¼ package chopped dates
½ cup chopped nuts
12 maraschino cherries
1 teaspoon vanilla

Cream butter and sugar. Add eggs, flour, dates, nuts, cherries, and vanilla. Mix. Spread in a shallow pan about ⅛ to ¼″ thick. Cook at 350° and cut into small squares while still warm. Sprinkle with powdered sugar.

Note: I think these are delicious and so easy.

Christmas Balls

¼ lb. candied green cherries
¼ lb. candied red cherries
6 slices candied pineapple
  (white, red and green)
7 oz. extra fine coconut
2 cups chopped pecans
4 tablespoons brandy
⅛ teaspoon salt
¼ teaspoon vanilla
1 can sweetened condensed
  milk

Chop and mix fruits and nuts. Add brandy and marinate. Combine with remaining ingredients. Let stand in ice box overnight for easier handling. Make into small balls and bake on greased pan at 350° for 10 to 15 minutes.

Date Balls

2 cups crispy rice cereal
1 well beaten egg
1 cup sugar
1 teaspoon vanilla
½ cup melted butter or
  margarine
1 cup chopped dates
1 cup chopped nuts
Powdered sugar

Mix all ingredients and boil 5 minutes. Shape into balls and roll in powdered sugar.

P.S. Pretty on a tea table and good.

Butter Cookies

1 cup butter
½ cup sugar
3 cups flour (scant)
1 teaspoon vanilla
Currant jelly or semi-sweet
chocolate chips

Cream butter and sugar, blend in flour and vanilla. Make into small balls and place on cookie sheets. Indent center and add either spoonful of jelly or a chocolate drop. Bake at 350° until light brown.

Note: These are very much like Cocoons but are prettier cookies. Makes a big lot. You do not have to grease the cookie sheets.

Coconut Macaroons

1 egg white
½ cup sugar
½ cup coconut
2 tablespoons melted butter
¼ teaspoon vanilla
½ cup oatmeal
⅛ teaspoon salt

Beat egg white until stiff, add sugar. Fold in other ingredients and drop on greased cookie sheet. Bake in moderate oven.

Note: Use regular oatmeal, not the quick cooking kind. Your kids will like these and they are so easy to make.

Pecan Cookies

4 eggs
Scant 2 cups sugar
2 cups flour
½ teaspoon baking powder
Pinch salt
2 cups chopped pecans
1 teaspoon vanilla

Mix eggs and sugar. Add flour which has been sifted with baking powder and salt. Add chopped pecans and vanilla. Drop about ½ teaspoon at a time on well greased cookie sheet. Bake at 325° for 10-12 minutes.

Note: You will note that these cookies do not have any shortening other than the pecans. Grease your cookie sheet very well.

Grandma's Oatmeal Cookies

½ cup sugar
½ cup butter
1 egg
3 tablespoons milk
½ cup oatmeal
1 cup flour
½ teaspoon salt
½ teaspoon soda
2 teaspoons allspice
1 cup raisins
½ cup chopped nuts

Cream sugar and butter, beat in egg and milk. Add oatmeal. Sift together dry ingredients saving out part of flour to dredge raisins and nuts. Mix together, adding nuts and raisins last. Drop by spoonful on greased cookie sheet and bake in 375° oven. Test one cookie first and if it flattens out in baking, add a little more flour. These are good for the kids and they will love them.

Note: Use regular oatmeal, NOT quick cooking.

Virginia's Lace Cookies

½ cup flour
¼ teaspoon baking powder
½ cup sugar
½ cup quick cooking oats
2 tablespoons heavy cream
2 tablespoons light corn syrup
1 tablespoon vanilla
⅓ cup melted butter

Sift flour, baking powder and sugar into a bowl. Add oats and mix well. Add cream, corn syrup, vanilla and melted butter. Mix well. Chill in refrigerator until thick. Roll into marble size pieces of dough. Place on ungreased cookie sheet, about 4" apart. Bake in center of oven at 325° until cookies spread and begin to turn light brown, about 10 minutes. Remove from oven and let stand until slightly cool, then remove from cookie sheet with spatula, working quickly.

P.S. Do not cook over 16 at a time as they must be removed quickly.

Oatmeal Cookies

1 cup shortening
½ cup brown sugar
½ cup sugar
2 egg yolks
1 cup sifted flour
1 cup quick oatmeal
6 oz. milk chocolate
2 tablespoons butter
Ground pecans

Cream shortening and sugars. Add egg yolks and dry ingredients. This makes a stiff dough. Spread on a flat cookie sheet and bake about 20 minutes at 350°. Cool about 10 minutes. Spread the chocolate which has been melted with butter over the top. Cover with ground pecans and cut into bars.

Note: These are wonderful.

Forgotten Cookies

1 egg white
¾ cup brown sugar
1 teaspoon vanilla
2 cups pecan halves (whole, do not cut)

Beat egg white until stiff, slowly add sugar while beating, then add vanilla. Fold in pecans. Drop by spoonfuls on cookie sheet lined with brown paper. Cook at 250° for 15 minutes. Cut off oven and forget cookies until they are dry. It takes several hours.

P.S. Easy and good. You can substitute chocolate chips for pecans, but I don't think they are as interesting.

Peanut Butter Cookies

1¾ cups flour
½ cup shortening
½ cup sugar
2 eggs
1 teaspoon vanilla
1 teaspoon soda
½ cup peanut butter
½ cup light brown sugar

Mix and bake on greased cookie sheet for 10 minutes at 375°.

Note: This dough can be kept in ice box and cooked as desired. The kids will like these cookies.

Brandy Rolls

¼ cup white corn syrup
¼ cup molasses
½ cup butter
1 cup sifted flour
⅔ cup sugar
½ teaspoon ginger
2 tablespoons brandy
Whipped cream

Heat corn syrup and molasses to boiling. Remove from heat and add butter. Sift together flour, sugar and ginger. Add gradually to molasses mixture. Mix well and add brandy. Drop by *half* spoonful 3″ apart on greased cookie sheet. Bake 10 minutes in oven that has been pre-heated to 300°.

Remove from oven and loosen cookies one at a time and roll over the handle of a wooden spoon. Slip off and fill with whipped cream when cool.

P.S. Work fast and don't worry about your hot hands. They are worth it!

Fruit and Nut Rolls

½ cup shortening
2 cups sifted flour
4 teaspoons baking powder
½ teaspoon salt
½ cup milk
1 egg
Melted butter
Sugar
Raisins
Chopped nuts

Cream shortening and flour which has been sifted with baking powder and salt. Add milk and egg, beaten together. Mix, working as little as possible. Roll very thin on board, spread with melted butter, sprinkle with sugar and cover with raisins and chopped nuts. Roll and cut in 1″ pieces. Put on greased cookie sheet and bake at 375°.

Note: These are good. When you cut into pieces, press together so filling will stay in.

Holiday Fruit Cookies

½ cup shortening
1 cup brown sugar
1 egg, beaten
1¾ cups sifted flour
½ teaspoon salt
½ teaspoon soda
1 cup sour cream
¾ cup candied cherries
¾ cup chopped dates
1 cup chopped pecans

Cream shortening, add sugar, cream well. Add well beaten egg. Sift flour before measuring and stir in with salt and soda. Add sour cream then fruits and nuts. Drop by spoonful on greased pan. Cook at 375°.

Note: Small fruit cakes.

Graham Cracker Cookies

Box of graham crackers
½ cup margarine
½ cup sugar
Chopped pecans

Break crackers in halves and put on buttered cookie sheet. In medium sized saucepan, melt margarine. When melted, add sugar. Stirring constantly, boil three minutes. Cover top of graham crackers with sugar mixture and smooth it on. Sprinkle with chopped pecans. Bake in 325° oven for 11 minutes. Remove from cookie sheet immediately and put on waxed paper.

P.S. Use your pastry brush to spread on sugar mixture. These are good, easy to make, and keep well.

Date Popovers

½ cup butter
1½ cups flour
1 cup grated sharp cheese
Red pepper and salt to taste
Stuffed dates

Cream butter, cut in flour and cheese and seasoning. Roll thin on floured board and cut into small rounds. Place a stuffed date on one side of round and cover with other side. Press with fork. Bake at 400° until light brown.

Note: These are lovely for teas, coffees or cocktail parties. I like to make mine small and put ½ date in them.

Ice Cream Cookies

½ cup butter
½ cup sugar
1 egg, well beaten
¾ cup all purpose flour
1 teaspoon vanilla
Pecan halves or almonds

Cream butter, sugar and salt. Add egg. Beat thoroughly. Add vanilla and flour. Make into small balls. Put on cookie sheet about 2″ apart. Press a pecan half or almond on top of each. Bake at 350° for 10 to 15 minutes. Cool on cake rack.

Ice Box Cookies

1 cup melted butter
2 cups brown sugar
2 eggs
½ teaspoon salt
3½ cups flour
1 teaspoon soda
1 cup chopped nuts

Mix butter and sugar, add eggs. Sift together dry ingredients and add with nuts. Shape into two rolls. Chill overnight in ice box. Slice *very* thin and bake at 375° on buttered cookie sheet.

Note: This dough may be kept in ice box for several days and cooked as desired. Will keep indefinitely in the freezer and is nice to have on hand for unexpected company.

Press Cookies

1 cup shortening
¾ cup sugar
1 egg
1 teaspoon vanilla
2¼ cups sifted flour
⅛ teaspoon salt
¼ teaspoon baking powder

Cream shortening, add sugar gradually, add unbeaten egg and vanilla. Add sifted dry ingredients. Press on cookie sheet and bake at 350°.

P.S. This is in case you have lost the book that came with your cookie press - I did!

Sand Tarts

1 cup sugar
⅔ cup *butter*
2 eggs
Flour
1 teaspoon soda
Pecan halves
½ cup sugar
2 tablespoons cinnamon

Cream sugar and butter. Add eggs and enough flour to make soft dough that can be rolled out very thin. Add soda which has been dissolved in 1 teaspoon boiling water. Roll *very, very* thin on well floured board. Cut with round cookie cutter and put on greased cookie sheet. Glaze top with egg white that has been slightly beaten with a little water. Mix cinnamon and sugar. Put pecan half in center of cookie and sprinkle top with cinnamon and sugar. Bake at 375° Makes 5 or 6 dozen cookies.

P.S. Our traditional Christmas cookies. Dad's favorite.

P.P.S. You have to use a spatula to put them on the cookie sheet as they should be paper thin. They keep for weeks in a cake tin.

225

Soft Sugar Cookies

1 cup soft butter
2 cups sugar
2 eggs
4 cups flour
1 teaspoon soda
1 teaspoon baking powder
¾ teaspoon grated nutmeg
¾ cup sour cream
2 teaspoons vanilla

Cream butter and sugar. Add eggs and stir in thoroughly. Add sifted dry ingredients alternately with sour cream and vanilla. This dough can be either dropped from a spoon on a buttered cookie sheet or rolled into flat cookies. Bake in 425° oven.

Note: It does not take long to bake these cookies and they have to be watched carefully. They are delicious cookies. If you do not like the flavor of nutmeg, substitute cinnamon. Unusually good!

Toffee Cookies

1 cup butter
1 cup sugar
1 egg, separated
1 teaspoon vanilla
2 cups flour
¾ cup ground nuts

Cream butter and sugar. Add beaten egg yolk and vanilla. Add flour and beat well. Dough will be stiff. Spread as thin as possible on large 12x18" cookie sheet. Glaze top with lightly beaten egg white and sprinkle with ground nuts. Bake 1 hour at 250°. Cut into small squares immediately as they are too crisp to cut when cool.

*Note: An **old** recipe but still delicious!*

Spiced Cookies

1 lb. seedless raisins
½ lb. candied cherries
½ lb. candied pineapple
1 lb. chopped nuts
½ cup Bourbon
1 cup sugar
⅔ cup butter
2 eggs
2 cups flour
1 teaspoon baking powder
1 teaspoon cinnamon
1 teaspoon soda
1 teaspoon clove
1 teaspoon allspice
1 teaspoon nutmeg
1 teaspoon ginger

Soak fruit and nuts in Bourbon. Cream sugar, butter and eggs. Add flour and baking powder sifted with spices. Mix with fruit mixture. Drop by spoonfuls on buttered cookie sheet and bake at 375°.

P.S. Spiced cookies or you could say "spiked" cookies!

P.P.S. You have to watch these carefully while baking because they brown quickly.

Sugar Cookies

1 cup sugar
¾ cup oil
1 cup powdered sugar
1 cup softened butter or
   margarine
2 eggs
4 cups flour
1 teaspoon soda
1 teaspoon cream of tartar
1 teaspoon salt
1 teaspoon vanilla
Sugar

Cream sugar with oil and powdered sugar. Add softened butter, eggs and flour which has been sifted with soda, cream of tartar and salt. Mix well and add vanilla. Chill. Make 1″ balls, flatten with bottom of shot glass on greased cookie sheet. Sprinkle with sugar and bake at 350° until light golden.

P.S. This makes a very big batch of cookies. I flatten mine and press the edges with the prongs of a fork. Edges brown and they are very pretty. I think they are really great!

Old Fashioned Taffy

2 cups sugar
¾ cup water
¼ cup vinegar

Put ingredients in saucepan and cook to 265° on candy thermometer. Pour on buttered platter and when cool enough to handle, pull until white and brittle.

P.S. I remember making this at my grandmother's house, and I still remember my burned hands. Be sure and butter your hands well before pulling—it's fun!

English Toffee

2 cups butter
1 lb. sugar
½ cup chopped pecans
12 oz. chocolate bits

Cook butter and sugar, stirring constantly, until mixture is the color of peanut butter. Pour mixture onto buttered cookie sheet Sprinkle chocolate bits on top of hot mixture and spread evenly. Sprinkle with chopped pecans. When cool, break in small pieces.

P.S. The original recipe said, "put a jar of peanut butter on the stove and when mixture reaches that color, it is done". This was before the day of candy thermometers. Awfully good.

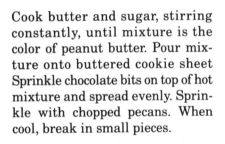

Chocolate Covered Coconut Candy

2 lbs. powdered sugar
1 (7 oz.) package coconut
2½ cups toasted pecans, chopped in blender
1 cup margarine
1 can sweetened condensed milk
4 oz. German sweet chocolate
½ cake paraffin (2 oz.)

Mix first 5 ingredients together. Chill. Roll in balls and dip in chocolate and paraffin that have been melted together in double boiler. Use toothpick to dip balls.

Pralines

1 cup brown sugar
1 cup white sugar
1 tablespoon butter
3 tablespoons boiling water
1 teaspoon vanilla
1 cup whole pecans

Put sugars, butter and boiling water in saucepan and boil for *1* minute. Remove from fire and add vanilla and pecans. Beat 1 or 2 minutes. Place by spoonful on aluminum foil while still runny. Yield should be about 18 pralines.

P.S. Do not beat too long or they will become grainy.

P.P.S. These are much better than the ones you buy in New Orleans.

Chocolate Fudge

2 oz. bitter chocolate
½ cup water
⅔ cup milk
2 tablespoons butter
2 cups sugar
2 tablespoons corn syrup
1 teaspoon vanilla

Mix together all ingredients except vanilla and cook until mixture reaches 230° on the candy thermometer. Cool and beat until creamy. Add vanilla and drop on greased platter.

P.S. When we were young and did not have TV or movies, we entertained our dates by making fudge. This was my favorite recipe.

Chocolate Truffles

¾ cup pecans
6 oz. semi-sweet chocolate
⅓ cup heavy cream
1 egg white
1⅓ cups powdered sugar
2 tablespoons Grand Marnier
   or rum
Chocolate decors

Butter a 9″ square pan. Chop pecans in food processor with steel blade until fine. In small saucepan, combine chocolate and cream. Stir over low heat until chocolate melts. Remove from heat and add pecans, egg white, sugar and flavoring. Stir well with wooden spoon. Pour into buttered pan and refrigerate overnight. Cut into small squares, roll into walnut size balls with your hands and roll balls in chocolate decors. These keep well in the refrigerator or freezer.

P.S. I hate to make these for certain people who are dieting and can't resist eating a few!

Peanut Brittle

2 cups sugar
1 cup water
1 cup corn syrup
⅛ teaspoon salt
2 cups raw peanuts
1 teaspoon soda

Cook together the sugar, water, syrup and salt until mixture forms a *hard* ball in cold water. Add the peanuts and stir until they are thoroughly parched. Remove from heat and add soda. Pour on greased marble slab until cold.

Note: This was my grandmother's recipe for peanut brittle. Finding a marble slab to pour it on is not easy these days. If you don't have one, use a greased cookie sheet or greased stainless steel counter top.

Christmas Orange Pecans

1½ cups sugar
½ cup water
Grated rind of 1 large orange
3 tablespoons orange juice
Pinch of salt
12 oz. pecan halves

Boil sugar and water until mixture spins a long thread or forms a hard ball when dropped in water. Remove from heat, add orange rind, juice and salt. Beat until creamy. Add pecans and pour on greased platter. Separate pecans.

Crunch

2 cups finely chopped
  almonds
1 cup butter
1¼ cups sugar
2 tablespoons light corn syrup
2 tablespoons water
1 (12 oz.) package chocolate
  chips

Spread almonds in shallow pan, toast in moderate oven until golden. Melt butter in large, heavy saucepan, add sugar, corn syrup and water. Cook, stirring often, to hard crack stage when dropped in cold water. Stir in 1 cup of almonds. Pour quickly on buttered cookie sheet, cool completely. When set, turn out on waxed paper. Spread half of melted chocolate on top. Sprinkle with half of remaining almonds. Let set, turn and do same to other side. Let set and break into pieces.

P.S. It takes a long time to cook the sugar mixture. It will be about the consistency of peanut butter when done. It is very good and keeps a long time. When you pour hot mixture on cookie sheet, shape as well as you can into an oblong.

P.P.S. Hard crack is 255° on candy thermometer.

Candied Grapefruit Peel

Peels of 3 grapefruit
1½ cups sugar
½ cup water

Soak the peels in water overnight. Cut into narrow strips with scissors. Put in saucepan, cover with water and bring to boil. Let boil a minute or two, and pour water off. Repeat this four times. Put sugar and water in large aluminum pan and boil until it makes a syrup. Add grapefruit peels which have been well drained. Let cook in syrup until syrup just about crystalizes. Put strips on waxed paper and when cool enough to handle, roll each strip in granulated or powdered sugar.

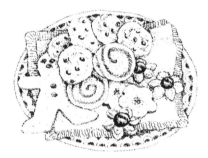

Note: This is time consuming as it takes time to prepare the strips and also they must be spread out on the waxed paper when they are done to have nice shapes. They are good, though!

Chocolate Candy Barbara

2 tablespoons melted paraffin
4 oz. German sweet chocolate
12 oz. butterscotch morsels
1 cup toasted pecans, broken
   in halves

Place paraffin in double boiler. When melted add the chocolate. Mix together until smooth. Add butterscotch morsels gradually, stirring until smooth. Remove from heat and add pecans. Mix well, cool slightly and drop by spoonfuls on waxed paper.

Mints

2 cups sugar
½ cup water
¼ teaspoon cream of tartar
1 tablespoon peppermint
  extract
Food coloring

Put sugar, water and cream of tartar in saucepan and boil until it forms a soft ball in cold water. Take off fire and without stirring, cool. Add peppermint and beat until a hard mass. This takes a lot of beating and you must beat until it is a clear white and formed mass. Melt in the top of a double boiler until it can be dropped from a teaspoon into small mints. Keep over heat while dropping. Color any desired color with a few drops of food coloring. When the syrup begins to get hard to drop easily from a spoon, add a little hot water from the bottom of the boiler.

P.S. Drop mints on a stainless steel top or on waxed paper. When mints harden, they will slip off the surface easily. Do not stack as they will melt.

P.P.S. This is the recipe I always use for Christmas mints. I divide the mixture and color some with green coloring and other with red.

Ice Box Fruit Cake Candy

1 lb. vanilla wafers, crushed
1 (7 oz.) pkg. flaked coconut
2 cups toasted pecans
1 cup raisins
1 (4 oz.) jar maraschino
  cherries, chopped
½ cup sweetened condensed
  milk, approximately

Crush vanilla wafers fine in blender. Mix dry ingredients together and add milk and a little juice from cherries. Pat into a roll and wrap in waxed paper. Makes about 4 rolls. Freeze and slice thin when serving.

233

Divinity

2½ cups sugar
½ cup water
¼ cup white corn syrup
2 egg whites, beaten stiff
1 teaspoon vanilla

Mix sugar, water and corn syrup. Cook over moderate heat until mixture forms a soft ball in cold water. Pour mixture very slowly over beaten egg whites, beating constantly. Add vanilla and beat until mixture holds its shape when dropped from spoon on waxed paper.

P.S. The secret of making this good is to start your egg whites beating about the time you start syrup boiling. It takes a very short time for syrup to cook so have everything ready. Pour syrup **very** *slowly into stiff egg whites. When you have 3 or 4 tablespoons of syrup left, put back on stove and let come to a boil and add slowly. I often use a buttered dish or dishes instead of wax paper to drop it on. Sometimes I decorate with a pecan half or crystalized red or green cherry. You can color the candy pink or green with coloring before dropping. I love it!*

P.P.S. This was my mother's recipe for Divinity. I try to make it just like she did for hers was always perfect.

Eggs separate easier when Cool —

Lagniappe

Cranmerry Berry Ice

1 package cranberries
1 cup water
½ cup orange juice
⅓ cup lemon juice
Sugar to taste
1 (8 oz.) bottle ginger ale
2 teaspoons grated orange
 rind

Cook cranberries with water until tender. Put through sieve, getting as much of the pulp as possible. Add orange juice, lemon juice and sweeten to taste. Add ginger ale and grated orange rind. Freeze. Several hours before serving, put in electric mixing bowl or food processor and beat until smooth. Fill sherbet cups and refreeze. Serve with meal instead of cranberry sauce.

Note: This means Christmas to my family. I dreamed this recipe up one Christmas and it is a favorite, not only for our family, but for many of our friends. Nick named it when he was three years old. He couldn't pronounce it very well but he surely could eat it, and still can!

Hot Fruit Casserole

12 almond macaroons
1 (8½ oz.) can chunk pineapple
1 (16 oz.) can apricots
1 (16 oz.) can peaches
1 (16 oz.) can pears
1 (6 oz.) bottle maraschino
 cherries
½ cup brown sugar
½ cup sherry

Drain fruit. Line baking dish with macaroons. Layer with drained fruit. Top with cherries, sprinkle with brown sugar and sherry. Bake in 350° oven until well heated.

P.S. This is better if you refrigerate overnight before baking.

P.P.S. This is a nice luncheon dish. Also good with pork or beef roast.

Hot Sherried Fruit

1 (8 oz.) can pineapple chunks
1 (16 oz.) can peach halves
1 (16 oz.) can pear halves
1 (16 oz.) can apricot halves
1 (15 oz.) jar apple rings
½ cup butter
2 tablespoons flour
½ cup light brown sugar
1 cup sherry

Drain fruit, arrange in layers in casserole. Arrange apple rings on top.

Cook sauce in double boiler until thick and smooth. Pour hot sauce over fruit. Cover and refrigerate overnight or for several days. Bake at 350° for 30 minutes.

P.S. So good with chicken or turkey!

Lenora's Cheese Soufflé

3 tablespoons butter
¼ cup flour
1⅞ cups milk
1 cup grated cheese (packed)
6 egg yolks, beaten
1 teaspoon prepared
  mustard
2 drops Worcestershire
Dash red pepper
6 egg whites, beaten

Make white sauce, melting butter, blending flour and adding milk slowly. Cook until bubbly, bring to boil, stirring constantly and boil one minute (time it). Remove from heat and add cheese. Stir until it melts. Beat egg yolks until thick. Add cheese mixture after it has cooled slightly. Season with mustard, Worcestershire and red pepper. Let cool. Beat egg whites until stiff and fold into cheese mixture with wire whisk. Pour into well greased soufflé dish. Put in pan with about an inch of water and bake at 300° until knife inserted in center comes out clean.

P.S. This is a great soufflé but be ready to eat when it is ready – or else!

Fettucini Alfredo

½ lb. wide egg noodles
1 tablespoon vegetable oil
¾ cup heavy cream
4 tablespoons sweet butter
½ cup freshly grated
  Parmesan cheese
Salt and pepper to taste

Cook noodles in boiling water with oil until done. Drain. Combine cream, butter, cheese, salt and pepper and simmer until thickened. Place noodles in attractive bowl, pour sauce over and toss until well combined. Serve with extra Parmesan cheese.

Spaghetti with Meat Sauce, Alberta

¼ cup oil
3 large onions, chopped
1 large bell pepper, chopped
2 lbs. ground beef
4 cloves garlic, minced
1 large can whole tomatoes
3 cups water
1 tablespoon chopped parsley
1 tablespoon Italian seasoning
2 teaspoons salt
½ teaspoon pepper
1 lb. spaghetti
Parmesan cheese, grated

Sauté onions and peppers in oil. Add beef and garlic and brown. Add remaining ingredients except spaghetti. Cook 2½ hours until thick. Add water as needed. Cook spaghetti according to package directions, drain and serve with sauce and Parmesan cheese.

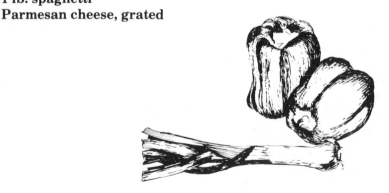

Quiche

9" pie shell, baked
10 slices cooked bacon,
  crumbled
⅝ cup Swiss cheese, grated
⅝ cup sharp Cheddar cheese,
  grated
4 eggs
½ pint heavy cream
Salt to taste

Evenly distribute bacon and cheese over the bottom of the baked pastry shell. Beat eggs, mix well with cream. Pour over bacon and cheese. Lightly salt. Bake in 325° oven for 40 minutes or until custard appears firm when gently shaken.

P.S. Other things can be substituted for the bacon—ham, shrimp, chopped olives, mushrooms, asparagus, etc.

P.P.S. Many people really like quiche. I don't.

Liederkranz Quiche

Preheat oven to 350°. Prepare 9" pastry shell. Bake 8 minutes and set aside.

1 lb. Italian sausage
1 lb. fresh mushrooms, sliced
1 (4 oz.) package Liederkranz
  cheese, cut up
1 cup heavy cream
4 eggs, well beaten
½ teaspoon salt

In large skillet, brown sausage stirring to break in small pieces. Remove from drippings. Add mushrooms. Cook and stir 5 minutes. Drain. In large bowl combine sausage, mushrooms, Liederkranz, cream, eggs and salt. Mix well. Turn into prepared pastry shell and bake 45 minutes.

P.S. Quiches are not among my favorite dishes, but I thought I should include a recipe or two for quiche lovers and this is a good recipe. You can substitute Gruyere if you prefer a milder cheese.

239

Fluffy Omelet

6 eggs
4 tablespoons butter

Prepare one of the following sauces in advance. To make your omelet, separate eggs. Beat whites in large bowl until stiff. In another bowl, beat yolks until thick and lemon colored. With wire whisk carefully fold yolks into whites. Put butter in 9 or 10″ skillet and place over low heat. When butter has melted, pour eggs into a skillet and cook *Do not stir!* Take a spatula and lift up sides of omelet and when bottom is brown, put skillet on middle rack of 300° oven. Let stay in oven until silver knife stuck into eggs comes out clean. Then remove from oven, take spatula, crease middle of omelet and fold onto warm platter. Cover with any sauce you like and serve immediately.

Sauces:

Using Basic White Sauce, add cheese, or chopped chicken, chopped ham, turkey, shrimp, or anything you like. You can make a Spanish omelet by cooking tomatoes, onions, olives, green pepper, etc. and pouring that over the omelet.

P.S. This was my mother's recipe. I don't think French omelettes compare with a good old fashioned fluffy omelet. This is a good meat substitute and a good way to use a little left over meat. You get a lot of mileage out of an egg this way!

Soufflé Sandwich, Ada Harvey

12 slices bread
6 slices cheese, medium or
  sharp
2 cans white crab meat
2 sticks butter
6 eggs
3 cups milk
½ teaspoon salt
½ teaspoon dry mustard
Corn flakes

Place six slices buttered bread in 9x13″ casserole. Cover with crab meat and cheese slices. Butter remaining bread and place over cheese. Beat eggs, milk, salt, and mustard together and pour over top. Cover with corn flakes and 1 stick butter melted. Refrigerate 24 hours and bake 1 hour at 350°.

Twenty-Four Hour Punch

1½ cups sugar
1 cup water
Juice of 1 dozen lemons
Lemon rinds
1 qt. Bourbon

Combine sugar and water and cook for 10 minutes. When cool add to lemon juice and rinds in a crock or large ceramic bowl. Add Bourbon and let sit overnight. Next day remove lemon rind and squeeze out juices. Serve chilled.

Note: This is really potent and has a good taste. It is nice to double, triple, etc. for a big party and then you don't have to mix drinks. We mix ours in an old-fashioned pottery churn left over from the good ole days.

Champagne Punch

1½ (6 oz.) cans frozen pink
   lemonade
1 bottle sauterne
3 cups cranberry juice
8 oz. club soda
2 bottles champagne

Dilute lemonade as per package instructions. Mix lemonade, sauterne and cranberry juice. Chill. Put in punch bowl and add club soda and champagne.

P.S. This is the recipe I worked out for a party for Jeanne. Had a headache for a week from tasting various mixtures! It's delicious. Prettier with pink champagne.

Fruit Juice Punch

1½ cups sugar
1 cup hot water
1 qt. orange juice
1 (46 oz.) can pineapple juice
1 (12 oz.) can apricot nectar
1 (6 oz.) can frozen lemonade
   concentrate
1 qt. ginger ale

Dissolve sugar in hot water. Add juices. When ready to serve, add ginger ale. Serves 25 to 30.

P.S. For the young and pure of heart! It is a good punch!

Basic Simple Syrup

2½ cups sugar
¾ cup white corn syrup
1¼ cups water

Combine in large saucepan and stir over low heat until sugar is dissolved. When clear, wash sides of pan down with a pastry brush dipped in cold water. Place lid on pan and cook 5 more minutes. Remove lid, increase heat and boil 5 minutes more without stirring. When cool, pour into jar and cover.

Eggplant

W

Z

Walker Enterprises

P.O. Box 1405   113 So. Lafayette St.
Starkville, Mississippi 39759

Please send me _____ copies of   _____
Southern Legacies @ $9.95 each
Plus postage and handling @ $1.50 per book   _____
Mississippi residents add 5% tax   _____

Enclosed is my check for . . . . TOTAL   _____

Please charge to my VISA ☐ Master Charge ☐ #_____

Expiration Date_____/_____ Signature_____

(Please print or type)

NAME_____

ADDRESS_____

CITY_____STATE_____ZIP_____

Please gift wrap ☐

Walker Enterprises

P.O. Box 1405   113 So. Lafayette St.
Starkville, Mississippi 39759

Please send me _____ copies of   _____
Southern Legacies @ $9.95 each
Plus postage and handling @ $1.50 per book   _____
Mississippi residents add 5% tax   _____

Enclosed is my check for . . . . TOTAL   _____

Please charge to my VISA ☐ Master Charge ☐ #_____

Expiration Date_____/_____ Signature_____

(Please print or type)

NAME_____

ADDRESS_____

CITY_____STATE_____ZIP_____

Please gift wrap ☐

Reorder Additional Copies